# EAST ANGLIAN
# YARNS

# EAST ANGLIAN YARNS

———✦———

*by*

*H. Mills West*

COUNTRYSIDE BOOKS
NEWBURY, BERKSHIRE

First Published 1992
© H. Mills West 1992

COUNTRYSIDE BOOKS
3 CATHERINE ROAD
NEWBURY, BERKSHIRE

ISBN 1 85306 191 3

Cover illustration by
Mark and Elizabeth Mitchels

Produced through MRM Associates Ltd., Reading
Typeset by Acorn Bookwork, Salisbury, Wilts
Printed by J W Arrowsmith Ltd., Bristol

# Contents

# Wagers of Yesteryear

There was never any problem of boredom among the local citizenry when the military occupied the barracks at Ipswich, Woodbridge and Bury St Edmunds. If it was not some dare-devil escapade it would be feats of physical prowess or personal challenges, even occasionally to duels, and always accompanied by wagers of breathtaking size.

There was the occasion during the spring of 1824, for example, when Captain Anderson of the Ipswich barracks undertook to perform what was called a walk, trot and gallop match. Probably with a good deal of experience of such competitions, the gallant captain maintained that he could, and would for a decent purse, walk his horse (named Mask) for three miles, trot three miles and gallop three miles all within the space of 50 minutes. Promised a substantial purse of 200 guineas and with a great deal of side-betting by all and sundry, the captain ensured that the event would become one of the most eagerly anticipated for years.

By early May of that year all preparations were complete, the course marked, the horse Mask brought to the peak of fitness and everyone ready for the great event. At that time the experts on horseflesh and horse speeds were legion but so delicately balanced were the prospects of success or failure that few could feel certain what the outcome would be. On the appointed day crowds of people thronged the Colchester road to witness the race. Many a golden guinea changed hands and many an old-fashioned timepiece was brought from waistcoat pockets and anxiously checked as the captain took his place with Mask at the starting point.

The three mile walk was made first, with Mask stepping out well and now and again looking likely to break into a trot but this was immediately corrected by the rider and no one felt that the rules had been broken. It took exactly 29 minutes for the walk, leaving only 21 minutes for the remaining six miles. In the brisk trot that came next Captain Anderson achieved the three miles in just under twelve minutes. It was still an even bet. Everything depended on the last leg of the match and how much speed Mask could summon in a gallop. With excitement at its height the captain made the headlong dash and brought Mask steaming to the winning post with just 30 seconds to spare.

The achievement brought to mind another substantial wager made on the memorable effort of Lieutenant Fairwin of the Militia some years before. In November, 1804, Lieutenant Fairwin set out on his self-imposed feat of endurance, this time on foot. He claimed that he would walk 60 miles in 14 successive hours. A mile-long course was set up along which he had to travel backwards and forwards 60 times while closely watched by appointed monitors. Lieutenant Fairwin started off at two o'clock in the morning and made good speed until daylight and also through the following morning so that the twelve hour mark at two o'clock in the afternoon showed that he had made an average of 4½ miles an hour. After that time his pace slackened a little, he broke off once or twice to enter an adjacent cottage for refreshment but still kept an average of 4 miles an hour. The last few miles of this lonely marathon were completed with all the signs of great fatigue and took 17 minutes to each stretch but Fairwin still managed to finish the 60 miles and with 27 minutes of the 14 hours to spare. The first to congratulate him was the colonel who was believed to be the other party to the wager.

In 1818, a civilian walker of some renown gave out that he was prepared to walk a quarter of a mile every quarter of an hour for 1000 hours, a feat which he succeeded in achieving in 'good spirits' according to the reports. The arrangement required a bell to be fixed at the end of his regular walk which he was required to ring. He was also monitored by two men during the hours of darkness and one man in the daytime.

Much more daunting was the extraordinary feat of a Mr Townshend who was not only a great walker but also a great showman and always crowned his many achievements with a great deal of spectacular excitement. In July 1824 Mr Townshend undertook to travel on foot from Ipswich to Halesworth and back again each day for ten days, a distance of 64 miles a day. To many of those who weighed up the possibilities of such a challenge, it seemed an impossible task and as each day passed a kind of hysteria grew among local people until they could scarcely contain themselves to await the thrilling finish. Finish Townshend did, arriving in Ipswich on the final day in the style of a conquering hero. From the outskirts of the town to the Cornhill he was led by the town band playing the most triumphant martial music and followed by crowds the like of which the streets had seldom seen. At the Cornhill, Townshend was met and congratulated by dignatories and feted by the common folk. He appeared on a first floor balcony overlooking the crowd and made a speech in which he made it clear that he was by no means overtaxed physically by the achievement. While the bells of St Mary-le-Tower pealed out in acclamation of this one-time superstar, he issued a challenge to anyone to beat his record.

Wagers were usually the cause and betting the inevitable accompaniment of such feats but they were also applied to any matters of chance that took the punter's fancy. One of the most profitable wagers ever made was that entered into by a captain of the local military while on a visit to London. It was at a time when there was much speculation as to the state of the King, George III. A spate of gloomy rumours had it that he was about to die, sick in mind and body as he was. When the captain wondered, in the hearing of a group of London gentlemen, if it was possible to be so certain of the King's death merely from a flood of hearsay, it became a matter of honour for the Londoners to put the captain in his place and repeat their conviction that the King would not recover from his present illness and must soon die.

Although the captain had no way of knowing any better than anyone else about the King's health, he was able to judge that the popular forecast was made from the slimmest of facts and arose from the sheer volume of rumour. When he heard again the pronouncement of the King's imminent death, the officer was piqued into wagering that the King would live. A London merchant, in his turn was prepared to accept the wager. An agreement was quickly made whereby the captain would hand £20 to the merchant at once and receive in return a guinea a day for so long as the King lived. The contract was drawn up, signed and witnessed and it must have been the subject of many a scene of contention in the future for the King persisted in living for another 30 years.

Occasionally the military gentlemen engaged in duels. The outcome was usually very undramatic and unbloody. The marksmanship, for example, of two officers who had disagreed over a game of billiards, provides no great confidence as to their fate if ever they were face to face with a determined enemy. In the time honoured dawn encounter the two men – one a lieutenant of the Horse Guards and another an ensign in the West Suffolk Militia – came to the chosen venue in the gravel pit at the Ipswich Race Ground. They each fired three brace of pistols at a distance of ten paces and succeeded in missing each other completely. Apologies were offered and accepted and all ended amicably. A similar encounter took place between two officers at the Woodbridge Barracks when satisfaction for some slight or other required the use of pistols. In this case, one escaped unhurt while the other was wounded in the foot – whether from his own or his opponent's fire was never revealed.

# Self-Service, Old Style

The rich people had flour – the farmers and the millers had flour but the villagers had none. In that year of 1795 and particularly in the north and west of Suffolk, flour was more precious than gold and many people likely to starve for lack of it. It was a year when desperate men gathered in barns and cart sheds to seek ways of easing the hunger that lay like a plague on the countryside. In the end, those men were driven to seize what was then the staple of life. By law, the taking of flour was a heinous crime but here it was done in so controlled and equitable a way that, in the light of common sense and justice, most of the perpetrators escaped punishment.

Misfortunes had begun with the wretched weather of the previous year. There had been a mild winter followed by an equally unseasonable summer, with frosts in June, a long period of drought and then heavy autumn rains that made cultivation impossible. Throughout the year of 1794 there were infestations of green and black 'lice' that preyed on the crops. In the following year there was but half a crop of wheat and the small proportion that was suitable for bread became scarce and expensive. Poor people could not afford to buy the bread corn and became desperate as soon as their meagre hoard of gleanings was exhausted.

Some responsible farmers and local gentry recognised how serious the situation was and provided a limited measure of help by distributing a ration of flour at a reduced price. Mr Rabett of Bramfield Hall, for example, gave the 'industrious poor' four cauldrons of coal and sold them flour at eleven shillings a hundredweight or two shillings a stone. At Brandon and many villages in that area there were collections among the well-to-do that allowed them to share out a certain amount of flour at a shilling a stone. Dr Frere of Finnigham provided a dinner of beef and plum pudding for all the villagers as well as a considerable amount of coal and clothing.

But, all in all, it made little difference to the situation. As conditions worsened during the winter of 1794 to 1795 and the following spring, poor people became convinced that many farmers and millers were storing flour in barns and granaries to cause prices to rise. In the early summer a great crowd of hungry folk met outside the house of a Sudbury miller and shouted their demand for a reduction in the price of flour. When they received no satisfactory answer, the crowd moved to the mill. There was a wagon standing there with five sacks of flour in it and immediately there was a score of willing hands to haul the waggon to the market in Sudbury. With more restraint than one would expect of those with many hungry mouths to feed at home, the flour was weighed out with meticulous care and sold to the poor at what was considered to be a fair price. The money and the waggon and even the empty sacks were then returned to the miller. Next day, the crowd stopped a waggon containing four sacks of flour and, while the carter looked helplessly on, dealt with it in the same manner.

On another occasion, a mob of about 300 villagers stopped a waggon containing 20 sacks of flour and distributed it among themselves at a fair price of two shillings a stone. The money was collected and promptly taken with the empty sacks to the miller concerned. Having been trying to sell the flour at the excessive price of three shillings and five pence, the miller was less than happy with the forced sale at two shillings and threatened the deputation with the law. The difficulties of arresting 300 desperate villagers, together with the fact of widespread sympathy for their cause, made such a threat impossible to enforce. Many of those in official positions contented themselves with reproving the mob for their actions and advising them of the superior virtues of the potato over corn in the diet.

Not for the first time – or the last – the humble potato was thrust forward as a perfect and much-undervalued source of nutrition. No less a personage than a magistrate was setting a public example by using potatoes at every opportunity and was cutting his household's flour requirement by half. Such advice, well meaning as it may have been, did not impress country folk brought up to eat bread nor did it prevent a crowd gathering at Bures where it broke down the doors of a farmer's barn and took 29 coomb of wheat. The wheat was dragged away to the village centre and sold next day to those in most need in that area, each stone weighed out and paid for and the money returned to the farmer. In the reprehensible position of trying to hoard the corn for a higher price, the farmer had little choice but to accept.

Shortage of good bread corn had by this time caused a certain amount of adulteration in flour. Incensed by what seemed to be another trick of the millers, cottagers in the Wetherden area gathered in the village in indignant mood with the intention of marching to Stowmarket to protest at the quality and the price of flour. So militant did this group become that alarms were sent out and a detachment of the Queen's Bays turned out to accompany the marchers and keep order. In the end the protest simmered down when Stowmarket bakers demonstrated that the new flour mixture of wheat and barley could produce a bread of adequate quality.

Fortunately, the passing seasons now brought better weather and in the summer of 1796 a bulging harvest took away some of the bitterness between farmer and worker. There was flour again without stint and after the harvest the women flocked in to the fields to glean. The farmers, as usual in those days, had the last word.

No one was to enter any field for gleaning until it was completely cleared and not before eight o'clock in the morning or after seven in the evening. The church bells in the respective parishes would be rung at those times. Only women and children would be allowed to glean and no field should be entered by any other means than a proper gateway. As gleaning was an indulgence by farmers, they expected similar indulgent conduct from gleaners; the older and steadier women were expected to restrain the children and younger women and to see that fences were protected. In a veiled threat, the gleaners were given to understand that, 'a reasonable attention to these points would prevent the necessity of applying to a magistrate'. There was no wish to interfere with the right to glean but to prevent the improper conduct that had prevailed in late years.

It would be wrong to suggest that there was always gloom in rural life. Quite the opposite if the harvest was good, the domestic flour sack full and an excuse could be found for some jollification. Such an opportunity arose, just 20 years after the sad episodes of the flour shortage, at the downfall of Napoleon. The wars were over, the threat of invasion gone and in the days set aside for countrywide thanksgiving the people flocked to village greens and market squares in a commitment to pleasure. Everyone seems to have been involved from the least to the most lordly, both in the preparation and in the enjoyment of festivities, which in many villages continued for two whole days.

At Needham Market, for example, after the morning's excited preparations, about 600 people joined in a feast of roast beef and plum pudding with an endless supply of good ale. There was dancing and singing in the street and tea for all who desired it. At Easton there was a day breathless with entertainment and feasting. The gentry of the village joined with every one of the cottagers – about 300 in all – to rejoice and share the mountains of food. That the quality drank port while the poor drank 'Old Stingo' bothered no one. There was so much more to enjoy, with sports, dancing and games in an atmosphere of complete if sometimes bibulous conviviality.

Next day, the village of Easton determined to continue with the full measure of festivity and pushed 'Old Stingo' around

14

again in flowing mugs. Then there was more feasting and feats of skill in spinning matches and drawing matches, with a tug o'war across the river. In the evening there was dancing on the lawn at the rectory where at midnight an effigy of Napoleon was set up as a grand climax and contented villagers watched just for the pleasure of seeing it burn.

# From Culinary Acorn
# to Oak Tree

At the time that I knew Mr Ernest F Easto, he was a comfortably rotund gentleman with a genial temperament to match, looking forward to his retirement from the post of headmaster of what was then called an Area School. His long career in village schools, interrupted by foreign service in the Great War, had shaped a man so skilled in teaching that he could hold a class enthralled from the moment he entered the room. It was not EFE's only claim to distinction. He had, he said, planted an acorn. It was his own phrase, complete with the observation that his acorn grew into a mighty oak and I am sure that he gained a great deal of satisfaction from the thought.

The venue of the acorn planting was the village school of Henham-with-Wangford near Southwold, where Mr Easto was headmaster. His wife was on the staff of the same school. Like all village schools then, the pupils were of all ages and abilities, about 160 altogether from Henham and the villages around. Until the day when EFE left to join the forces overseas the husband and wife team had run the school with complete success. Now, with the war going on and little but bad news from the Front, there were new rules and new challenges. Mrs Easto met them immediately, particularly through her concern for food shortages and malnutrition. After a good deal of experimental cooking and costing of groceries, she instituted a series of lectures boldly called 'A Satisfying Meal for a Family of Five for One Shilling.' Country mothers, themselves experts in eking out wartime rations, were duly impressed by the practical demonstrations that accompanied the lectures. Among the many who attended was Mr W E Watkins, secretary of the East Suffolk Education Committee, who was keenly interested in the problems of wartime food and took away particulars of meals and their costs. A valuable friend and ally he turned out to be.

There is no doubt that at this point the cultivation of the soil began which was to nurture the future acorn. When Mr Easto was invalided home from France, he joined his wife in her investigations into the problems of making best use of short rations. Probably the Henham children were more fortunate than many others, being able to share in natural country produce but they were still affected by the general situation. Pupils who lived too far from school to go home for a mid-day meal usually brought a package of slices of bread covered with a scraping of margarine or jam. It was the sight of this diet as much as anything else that distressed the Eastos and very soon led to the thought that if a family of five could be provided with a hot meal for a shilling, surely the same could be done for children at school. By the same reckoning, a meal could be provided for a child each day for a week for the same amount.

It was a thought that teased Mr Easto during his convalescence. At that time it was a staggering proposition that a school should feed its pupils and as a matter of cold fact, completely impossible. How could they cook hot meals without any facilities, without utensils, crockery, cutlery? More important – could they get extra rations? And would the parents agree? Would the managers agree? Would the local authority look kindly on such an unheard-of experiment?

It took some months to overcome the obstacles, one at a time. Even then, the Eastos realised, it would all be for nothing if insufficient numbers of children came forward with their shilling. Using the utmost economy and ingenuity there would still have to be a minimum of 40 to 50 meals a day to keep the cash in balance. Despite the guarded approval of Mr Watkins and the local authority, it was made clear that there

17

would not be a ha'porth of assistance. Whatever happened, the scheme must not be supported by public funds.

It was mid October, with the war slowly fading behind but with food rationing still severe, when Mr and Mrs Easto decided it must be now or never for the project. There was a coal range in one of the classrooms which was fairly amenable if the wind was in the right direction and, in answer to a plea for help to Lord and Lady Stradbroke at nearby Henham Hall, masses of kitchen utensils had been donated. Children were enjoined to bring their own plate, knife, fork and spoon which they would have to wash themselves after use.

On the first day 60 children sat at their desks for the school meal and by the end of the week there were 80. Despite all the things that could have gone wrong, only minor mishaps occurred and such was the good report of the meals that parents gratefully handed out their shilling a week for the rest of the term and the terms following.

Over a two week period, this would be a typical series of menus:

| | |
|---|---|
| Monday – | Suet pudding and gravy, mashed potatoes and carrots |
| | Ginger baked squares and custard |
| Tuesday – | Meat and vegetable soup with bread |
| | Jam tart |
| Wednesday – | Meat and vegetable pie, with crust |
| | Suet pudding with jam or treacle |
| Thursday – | Shepherd's pie with gravy |
| | Currant pudding with custard |
| Friday – | Meat patties, potatoes, greens, gravy |
| | Treacle or jam roll |
| Monday – | Dumplings, potatoes, greens, gravy |
| | Treacle tart |
| Tuesday – | Sausages and mashed potatoes, with bread |
| | Rice pudding |

Wednesday – Irish stew, with bread and potatoes
Sultana cake and custard
Thursday – Cornish pasties and gravy
Date or fig pudding
Friday – Boiled meat roll with mixed vegetables
Apple patties and custard

These simple meals, provided at about the time of the Armistice in 1918, were the first cooked school meals in the country, the Eastos believed. No doubt present day nutritionists would find much to be critical of in the diet then offered but it seems to me to be a very good and well thought out arrangement under the circumstances. Restrictions were caused by the small allowance of rationed meat at 15 shillings a week (though it was regularly supplemented by unrationed bones and offal) and by the lack of adequate equipment which meant that if one course was baked the other must be boiled or steamed. There was no fuss about vitamins, calories and suchlike bogies that haunt our meals today but just the commitment to fill hungry stomachs with good, wholesome food. This the Eastos succeeded in doing, to everyone's satisfaction and especially their own as, after taking stock of progress after a few weeks, they found that they had made an average profit of sixteen shillings and eight pence a week. It was a sum beyond their wildest expectations and meant that in future they could employ a cook for ten shillings a week. There was great relief for all, no doubt including the local authority which would be wondering if the undertaking was interfering with the school's proper function.

The mighty oak was beginning to grow! A year after the meals started, Mr Watkins succeeded in persuading the local authority to make its first concession by placing a small ex-army hut in the playground fitted with the basic essentials of cooking range, copper and sink. By this time the neighbouring schools of Henstead and Ilketshall were ready to follow the pioneering Henham and gradually other schools followed with varying success. In those early days there was always a satisfying amount of voluntary support not only from parents and managers but also from Food Office officials and health visitors. The idea of feeding children at school grew steadily between the wars and in due course reached the eminence of being enshrined in the 1944 Education Act as an integral part of school life.

The tree was full grown. In his lonely retirement, having out-lived his wife and help-mate, EFE derived much comfort and satisfaction from contemplation of the mighty oak that had arisen from an acorn planted long ago in a tiny Suffolk school.

# True Daughter of Norfolk

Her story should be told again in local terms, because she was a true daughter of Norfolk, one of that select band raised and nurtured in country parsonages who left their secure home life to set the world to rights. There have been many such as Edith Cavell in East Anglia and something of their motives and their abiding affection for their home pastures has been voiced in immortal verse by Edith's contemporary, Rupert Brooke. They shared the same style of upbringing in a quiet vicarage, shared the same dedication to a cause and both died in exile, in the same year of 1915. Much of Rupert Brooke's poetry of nostalgia could be as well suited to Edith, for she loved Norfolk and the coast walks in particular. In the years of her dedication to helping and healing abroad she must have been sustained often by the memory of the sounds of sea birds and the wind rustling the reeds in lonely places far away, where there was 'gentleness and hearts at peace under an English heaven.'

Perhaps monuments and history books do a disservice to those whose lives were strong and vital. Yes, we say, we remember reading about Nurse Cavell but that was in the Great War and there have been other heroines since then in other wars. We know too that so much fiction about the work of underground movements has reduced the sharp impact that was once felt at her barbaric execution. Yet it is still within living memory that what seemed to be half the population of Europe and all the population of Norfolk stood in shocked silence and respect when she was brought on that belated journey home.

She had faced the firing squad calmly, conscious that she had served no other cause but that of caring for all that needed her help; but the shots that rang out shook the world. Perhaps it was true, as many have affirmed, that two of the greatest mistakes that Germany made in that war was the sinking of the *Lusitania* and the execution of Edith Cavell. Both events aroused the Allies to a new and fervent spirit of patriotism.

But this is a short recollection of a Norfolk girl rather than of a national figure – a glance at what a statue fails to show, of a simple, loving life in an environment of quiet discipline. It lasted but a short time, just for the first 17 years of her life, but long enough to give her the strength and zest to launch herself into the world and long enough to fill her life with memories until she returned at last to the silence of the fields. All that is inbetween – her dedicated work in Belgium and England and the events leading to the monstrous injustice of her death – all is already told in great detail in the pages of other books.

Edith was born at Swardeston, near Norwich, at the vicarage where her father was the incumbent, in December 1865. Her full name was Edith Louisa Cavell and she was the eldest of four children, receiving her education at home. In the years in which she grew up in the quiet, well-ordered vicarage at Swardeston she followed the usual whims and dreams of youth, reading and painting (for which she had a talent) and walking around the village in the course of helping in the good works expected of the clergyman's family. In some way too, it seems, she was preparing herself for the challenges of the future. The first sign of an unusual character came when she left the secure life at the vicarage and at the tender age of 17 launched herself into a series of pupil-teaching jobs at places as far apart as Somerset, Peterborough and London.

A small legacy that came her way when she was 23 allowed her to travel for a time on the continent, where she had her first view of nursing conditions there, a sight that appalled her. She was 30 years old when she entered the profession of nursing as a probationer but was so quickly advanced in the hierarchy that she was soon in charge of hospitals in the most depressed areas of London. In 1906, at the invitation of a Dr

Depage of Belgium, she accepted the task of introducing more efficient methods into Belgian nursing.

As it happened, Edith was home again on vacation in her beloved Norfolk when war was declared and she immediately returned to the Belgian hospital to nurse Allied and German wounded alike without concern for anything but her desire to help others. It was in the same spirit that she became a link in the chain of contacts that helped British soldiers to escape from imprisonment or death at the hands of the enemy.

Nurse Cavell was executed at two o'clock on the morning of the 12th of October 1915 and the torch of patriotism lit that day continued to burn fiercely throughout the years of the war. As soon as the war was over, a monument was erected in Tombland, Norwich and unveiled by Queen Alexandra, while arrangements were made to bring the nurse's body home.

There have been state funerals in the past of impressive proportions but never such a voluntary expression of grief, as that which accompanied Nurse Cavell's cortege. People had waited four years to pay their homage and from the moment that the slow train left Brussels on a spring day in 1919 there were groups of people assembling in respect. In fields beside the line, workers stood with heads bared. Once in England, there was a solemn progress to London and Westminster Cathedral for a service of commemoration, and then the real homecoming to Norwich with the sort of people she loved welcoming her home in their thousands. Soldiers carried the coffin to the cathedral as slow marches were played by the bands of the Royal Scots and the Norfolk Regiment. It was the coming home of a Norfolk village girl as a national heroine, back to the earth and the sky and the quiet love that had moulded her.

# A Crime Without Reason

What do these four quiet villages – Long Melford, Peasenhall, Polstead and Acton – have in common? The answer is murder. They all carry the abiding scandal of long-past murder most foul, though the crimes themselves have little similarity. Perhaps the one least known, at Acton near Sudbury, is the most intriguing, not so much as to who-done-it as to why it was done at all. The two principals in the drama were an ordinary young couple, sweethearts from childhood, both of them well known and popular in the village. Both had relatives living nearby with whom they were on open and friendly terms and often joined them in going to church on Sundays.

Catherine and John Foster had been together practically from the day that they first went to the village school. When they left school at 14 they continued their friendship as sweethearts and were courting in a proper and time-honoured way for three years. Both were employed during that time, Catherine in respectable domestic service, John in apprentice-ship with Mr Meekings at Chilton.

On October 28th 1846, when Catherine was 17, the couple were married. She was now Catherine Foster, a name that would reach the ears of millions of people in a very short time. Like many other servant girls she saw marriage as an end to working for other people and she devoted herself to looking after her husband. The couple were fortunate in that there were no problems about accommodation. They moved in with Catherine's mother, Maria Morley, in a small cottage and it seemed it was Catherine's pleasure to keep the place clean and tidy, as her mother went out each day to do washing. Nothing could have been more cosy or promising of the future for a young couple. Yet from the beginning, things seem to have got out of tune. In the same week in which she had been married, Catherine went to Pakenham and stayed there for four days with her aunt. From a remark that she made to her aunt it appeared that she regretted leaving domestic service to. get married.

Perhaps it was just a tiff – nothing important. Yet, as Catherine resumed her domestic chores quite cheerfully in the cottage, some thought of violence must have awakened in her that quickly developed into an obsession carefully hidden by homely rectitude. It was only four months from the day of her wedding to the day, as bland and wifely-supporting as ever, she killed her husband by arsenic poisoning.

On that same fateful day Catherine had visited her mother-in-law in what was to all appearances a friendly social call as befitted her role as a new matron. She spent some time on the errand, so much so that at five o'clock she suddenly bestirred herself and told John's mother that she must hurry home to get his meal ready. She was going to make dumplings – John was very partial to dumplings. 'This is Tuesday,' she said, 'I always make dumplings on Tuesdays.' It seems to have been an ordinary, cheerful meeting between the two women and yet there is a chilling thought in the idea of visiting her mother-in-law on the day that Catherine intended to take John's life. Was this village girl so full of venom that she could take satisfaction from planning such a situation or were her pleasant manners genuine and quite apart from the dark deed that she contemplated? Certainly she already had the arsenic in her possession.

The atmosphere of comfortable domesticity was resumed when Catherine arrived home from her visit. It was a quarter past five and time to set out the baking utensils on the kitchen table. Very soon, she had made dumplings for John, for John's younger brother who was eight years old, and herself. She and Thomas had their dumplings at once and were eating them when John arrived home from work at six o'clock. Catherine got up and gave him the dumplings she had saved for him. He had scarcely started to eat before he became violently sick and he staggered out into the yard to retch. At seven o'clock Catherine's mother came home from her day's washing to find John apparently desperately ill in bed. The women decided that there was no chance of contacting a doctor until the morning and thought that, with attention, he might soon recover.

Next morning Catherine set out to walk to Long Melford to tell Dr Jones. From the description that Catherine gave of the symptoms, the doctor concluded that it was a case of 'English cholera' of which there had been something of an epidemic. He made up powders of mercury, chalk and rhubarb for Catherine to take home and promised to call later. When he arrived at the cottage at five o'clock he found that John was dead.

Dr Jones had no reason to suspect foul play and gave a formal verdict on the certificate but informed the coroner as a matter of course. At the inquest the coroner ordered a post-mortem and any hopes of concealment that Catherine may have had were lost. Traces of arsenic were found in the body and at a later exhumation the finding was confirmed.

Evidence was soon coming forward that would convict Catherine. Thomas, the younger brother of John who was in the kitchen when Catherine was making the dumplings said that he saw her take a small packet from her apron and empty the contents into the mixing bowl, afterwards burning the packet. However dubious such a testimony seems to be, coming from a child of eight, it agreed with much of the other evidence of Catherine's guilt. Of all places, final condemnation came from the cottage's backyard and of all creatures from the neighbour's hens. Apparently the hens ran freely at the back of the group of cottages. When the neighbour saw part of a dumpling which had been thrown or dropped in the yard, she picked it up and crumbled it for the chickens. Some of the chickens died and were found to have arsenic in their crops.

Why did Catherine kill her sweetheart of so many years? No one could discover the reason and to the present time it remains a strange and puzzling tale, particularly as the trouble was strictly between the two and neither lovers nor relations were involved in any way. At the trial the facts were so damning that it took the jury only a quarter of an hour to reach the verdict of guilty. Catherine Foster was executed at Bury on 17th April 1847 and 10,000 people indulged their morbid curiosity in watching her die.

# East Anglia by Stages

In the severe flooding of 1796 the Norwich to Ipswich mails came to a halt at Scole, where passengers had to be put into boats. The mail itself was carried by boat and then by horseback to reach its destination. It was one of the many occasions when the mail coaches made journeys in almost impossible conditions and when the guard in his red hat and coat and armed with pistol, sword and blunderbuss, became a tower of strength to meet the challenge and see that the mails came through.

One such guard was George Beck of Ipswich, a 'shot-gun Charlie' of considerable proportions and even greater courage. After the flood that year and with Christmas approaching, George took it on himself to follow the custom and go round the Ipswich taverns in order to collect contributions for mail coach personnel and their dependants. It was a popular cause and George did very well, his box becoming more and more heavy and his senses less and less acute as he came to the last calling place realising that he had indulged in more than a moderate amount to drink. He sat down in a corner of the bar feeling very tired and handed the box to the landlady for safe keeping. After a few minutes he must have decided that he was well able to take care of the money himself and took the box back, held it in his lap and went to sleep. When he woke up the box had gone. George stormed and complained, vainly accusing customers and bartenders alike of robbing him but finding there was no chance of recovering the money.

It was said that after this, the friendly public servant became a changed character for a time, riding grimly on the coaches to Norwich or Yarmouth and giving no one any more help than was strictly necessary. The time soon came, however, when he was called upon to perform a rescue act that was far beyond the call of duty.

Both the Ipswich to Yarmouth coach and the Yarmouth to Ipswich coach had set out that day in their opposite directions despite the threat of difficult weather conditions. In driving snow the two coaches pushed on through deepening drifts as far as Great Glemham and here both of them stuck fast within sight of each other. A gang of 15 men arrived to try to dig them out but by this time the snow was piling up so rapidly that there was no hope of continuing the journey. Passengers and horses were taken off and accommodated nearby and George was left with the responsibility of the mail. Fortunately, it was contained in a single sack which he settled on his back and pushed off across country on foot. Road and field had become one white plain under the snow and George simply followed what he thought must be the right direction for Woodbridge. Floundering through ditches and across open fields he arrived at Woodbridge six hours later, his hands all but frozen to the sack and half dead from the cold and exposure.

Apart from such dedication, one of the most enlightening things about the 'slow' old coaching days of the last century is the realisation of the break-neck speed at which the journeys were accomplished. For example, the parcel mail between Ipswich and London which was inaugurated in 1887 was carried entirely by mail coaches and as punctually as they are today. The coach, with driver and guard, left Ipswich each evening by an exact schedule at 7.09 pm. At hostelries along the route fresh horses waited to take over from tired ones, a new driver was taken on and at 4.30 in the morning by the timetable the coach was expected to draw in at Mount Pleasant where the parcels would be sorted for a breakfast delivery.

By this time the hazards of the journeys were less by reason of highwaymen and footpads than by the extremes of weather.

It happened more often than was comfortable on wintry days that the mail coach had to be abandoned and the mail taken on horseback. On one occasion the guard of the Yarmouth coach which had left the road and landed in a snowdrift, commandeered a local post-chaise and continued with this as far as possible but later had to abandon this too and with a small band of men and horses succeeded in carrying the bags of mail across country to their destinations. The guard arrived 16 hours behind schedule 'much fatigued and bruised by repeated tumbles' and it was much regretted that the mail would be a few hours late.

Speed continued to be a prominent feature of the coach service until its decline through the arrival of the railways. There is a story of an epic race between two rival coaches all the way from London to Norwich, with so little between them at Scole that neither would stop at the coaching inn to take up passengers but left them gaping as they whipped up their horses for the last lap to Norwich. There was a devil-may-care attitude in many drivers, due partly to the increasing competition from other coach companies which required quicker and quicker journey-times and partly by sheer exuberance, a combination which frequently caused accidents. One regular driver on the Ipswich to Norwich run was likely to frighten his passengers out of their wits by driving at break-neck speed. Unfortunately, his flamboyant nature often led to quarrels and violence and he was eventually committed for manslaughter. By contrast there was the quiet-mannered Harry Rawlings who drove coaches from Ipswich to Eye and always sang to his horses as they pulled uphill.

Travel by stage-coach was, in the earlier days, an adventure accompanied by a considerable amount of discomfort and danger. At that time the journey from Aldgate to Norwich took two days, staying for the night at the Ipswich Great White Horse. This was the usual route, rather than that by Newmarket and Thetford, because of the dangers of highway robbery. In fact, it was said that by one route highway robbery was probable while on the other it was well-nigh certain. The wild stretch of heath between Newmarket and Thetford provided a perfect background for cut throats of all kinds.

In 1762 came the daring schedule of the Norwich Machine, which set out three times weekly for London from the Maid's Head. The challenge was taken up by the London and Ipswich post coaches which, in the following year, set up a standard ten hour journey between London and the Great White Horse of Ipswich. These ten hour journeys were a great breakthrough, making it possible to carry perishable goods to the metropolis and in the type of Dickensian pictures of stage coaches we are shown how fully this facility was used, with the vehicle laden with game, vegetables and fruit.

It is possible to accept, with a little disdain at their inferior speeds, that coaches were occasionally liable to have accidents, but it is almost incredible that farm carts and waggons too were so prone to disaster that it became illegal for anyone to ride on a waggon at all or to rest on the shafts of any farm cart. It must have been an extremely difficult law for tired carters to uphold when bowling along on lonely country roads but evidence that vigilant eyes were watching is shown by the number of people fined for what was considered to be a serious matter.

The watchers would be villagers who belonged to an association. In days when the law was neither so efficient nor so mobile, local societies were formed which not only helped to catch and prosecute felons, horse-thieves, highwaymen and rogues of all sorts, but also raised money in order to pay rewards for their capture. With an association in most rural villages, it was a foolish man who disobeyed the law in sight of his neighbours.

Misguided brothers Robert and John Hawkes of Crowfield, for example, were convicted of riding on an empty waggon at Coddenham and also of refusing to turn out of the way of a gentleman's chaise and were fined 20 shillings. At Wickham

Market, farmer Rush was fined the same amount for taking a ride in his own waggon.

It seems extraordinarily unfair to us nowadays, no doubt, but there was plenty of evidence that the practice was dangerous. Every week someone was killed through falling off the shafts of a waggon or farm cart, sometimes because a horse bolted, but more often because the driver was drunk. Reports of such accidents were brief and the coroner's verdict laconic – 'Killed by the wheel of a cart going over his head.'

# Drama in The Fens

You could count on the fingers of one hand the number of times that Lilian Brace had been outside the village and even then it was only the few miles to Wisbech for ribbons or shoes or material for a dress. Lilian dressed well by the standards of the Fenland village and, together with a natural charm of manner, it allowed her a slight superiority over other marriageable maidens. However, wedlock was not a state that she wanted to rush into headlong and three unexceptionable swains were rejected before, at the age of 23, she met someone who seemed able to share her desire for some degree of gentility. His boots were not covered by the black silt of the polders but clean and polished as befitted a man engaged in the business of buying and selling potatoes.

When the couple married, they shared the small house belonging to Lilian's mother and she was moderately content to accept that her husband must sometimes be away on business. While he was away she occupied herself in dress-making and cleaning the house thoroughly against the time of his return. It was only after some months, when she realised that she was pregnant, that Lilian began to fret, feeling that at this time she should have some support.

Under the circumstances, she was very glad to greet her old friend Mary Brant on Wednesday afternoons when Mary had a break from work. On this particular afternoon she had come cycling out from Wisbech with a bit of good news. She found Lilian sitting listlessly in the parlour which was so spick and span it could not have borne one more dusting or polishing. The state of maternity was given several minutes close attention by the two girls and then Mary let it out that she was excited about a circus coming to the area.

'Same one 'at come tew year ago – though yew din't go, did yer? Yew was tew busy courtin'. Yew ain't tew busy now, though, are yer? We oughter go an' see it t'gither, this time – that'd dew yew good, git yew out o' the house for a little while. Course, that ain't really a circus, more a menagerie wiv all kinds of animals an' things. What d'ye say? 'Sonely a couple o' miles.'

It took some persuasion to shake Lilian out of her domestic lethargy but in the end she agreed. On the very next Wednesday afternoon the two set off on their outing.

The menagerie was on a meadow beside the river, with the animals' cages within an enclosure that they had to pay to get in. There was a kind of stage near the cages where the strange beasts would be brought out for closer viewing and perhaps to do some tricks. Though Lilian did not feel too comfortable in the fetid atmosphere, she concentrated her mind on the animals and was fascinated by seeing so close the strange wild creatures she had only seen before in picture books. There were seals that did tricks and a llama from South America, a monkey with a tiny baby and so many whose names she did not know. The lions were promised as a final treat.

It was worth the journey and the discomfort, Lilian decided – it would be something to tell her husband about when he returned at the weekend. But then the lions appeared in their cage and a sudden excitement filled the air. It was not just the lions themselves but the way they were racing around their cage and how they were snarling at a man who appeared with a whip, that made the audience nervous.

The man with the whip seemed to be trying to calm the beasts. He called over his shoulder: 'Nothing to worry about, ladies and gentlemen. They'll be good as gold in a minute, do you see.'

The lions were not at all as good as gold. They were excited and aggressive. Another man appeared beside the first and the two regarded the agitated animals for some moments. Then the second man, who seemed to be the owner or manager of

34

the menagerie, turned to the small crowd of watchers and raised his hand.

'Ladies and gentlemen, as you can see, the lions are a wee bit excited. It's nothing to get worried about – all the animals here are fed and looked after as if they were our own children. Sometimes that ain't quite enough – they have instincts, these wild creatures that are beyond our understanding. From my long experience with putting animals and people in close proximity, I have learnt a few of those secrets. You may be surprised at this but I am going to ask if any good lady among you who is on the way to becoming a mother – who is expecting a baby?'

Lilian could scarcely believe it at first. All of a sudden the whole world was turning against her, pointing with accusing fingers. She was already stumbling towards the exit as she heard: 'if so . . . kind enough to leave, so that other people can enjoy the show.' Lilian felt the shame and the heat and the hostile looks of other women as she passed them and could not stand it any more. At the exit she fell in a dead faint.

When she recovered, she found Mary beside her looking very concerned and a group of women standing round.

'Shou'n't ha' come,' one woman was saying, to general agreement. 'Should ha' known,' said another for good measure. A woman of fierce demeanour thrust her face forward. 'It'll be marked!' She spoke in the tone of one who only dealt in irrefutable truths. 'You can be sure o' that. That child'll be marked!'

Mary spoke up for her friend. 'Tha's nonsense, that is. Tha's old-fashioned superstition. Them animals was jest hungry. They 'on't mark an unborn child.'

'Nonsense, is it?' rejoined the fierce woman. 'See this.' She dragged forward a younger woman near her and pulled down the scarf that covered her face. The girl quickly covered up again to hide the hare-lip of which she was ashamed.

'That ain't on'y hares at'll mark a child. You was frightened by them wild creatures – they'll leave a mark for sure.'

35

'She shou'n't oughter ha' come,' the women agreed. 'Wild animals they was, tew. She shou'n't never ha' come.'

Mary took Lilian's arm and tried to talk her into a cheerful mood as they walked home. Lilian was quiet, answering yes or no, thinking with dread of the long hours she would be alone with her thoughts after Mary had gone and there was nothing but horror ahead.

'Don't worry yourself about it,' ordered Mary, the good friend. 'I'll come over agin tomorrer, when I finish work.' So she did and many an evening after when Lilian might otherwise have felt like jumping into a dyke for despair. There were times when Mary came in like a fresh breeze, determined to drive away the clouds and other times when she just sat and held Lilian's hand. She was there, too, when the miscarriage happened a few weeks later.

# They Were
# Pulling For Victory

It happened on a winter's day long gone but one which I clearly remember. The weather was what you would expect in mid December, with flurries of snow and a threat in the sky of worse to come. Somehow, the winters seemed more desolate in the war years, mainly I suppose because there was very little to cheer up one's spirits. In 1943, the coming Christmas break was something to get over as quickly as possible – the festivities of pre-war days seemed a distant dream.

On this particular day the mobile gang directed by the county's War Agricultural Committee came to the farm where I was staying. There were about a dozen men, most of them old but with two or three young rejects from the forces among them. They stared at the acres of icy sugar beet leaves as if they would rather have been elsewhere than stuck in that huge field where the east wind cut across like a knife.

It was certainly a large field – one of those which, because of their size, had to be criss-crossed by tall poles to prevent enemy gliders landing. They were out of date now with the Germans occupied up to their necks in the bleak wastes of Russia but the poles remained, not being in anyone's way.

I saw everything that happened that day because I was engaged in clearing out one of the field's ditches that had become blocked. By the time for elevenses I had got to know some of the characters that made up the gang and incidentally a good deal of their opinions on the weather, this particular field, the foreman, sugar beet generally and 'them' who sent them out in such infernal weather. This was from the young men, the old men were silent and resigned.

37

After elevenses, the men packed their dinner bags under a hedge, tied on hessian sacks like aprons and waded in again into the icy rows of sugar beet. Each man worked between two rows, pulled the beet simultaneously with both hands, knocked each pair of roots together to shed some of the soil and then threw them down in orderly heaps. Now and then an old man would raise his head to see how far was the opposite hedge and a minute's respite. It was back-breaking labour but no one stopped. I noticed that the pattern of bent backs in the field hardly ever changed. Ahead of all was the huge ex-seaman they called Jumbo. He seemed to be the foreman's favourite, the pace setter. Jumbo rarely spoke except in monosyllables and these were better interpreted by the tone rather than the sense.

Behind Jumbo, in an impressive show of activity but never able to keep up was Bert who, unlike Jumbo, was ever ready to tell the uttermost details of his life. He was a Londoner, born and bred, who had brought his invalid wife into the country at the time of the blitz, he told me, and he could hardly wait for the war to end to get himself and his wife back to London. Far back in the field was the cripple Amos, who progressed crab-like between the rows and seemed to arouse the best in the natures of the hard-bitten members of the gang since they regularly sacrificed a few minutes respite under the hedge in order to help him finish his stretch.

When I returned to the field just before one o'clock after a hot meal in the farm kitchen, the men were huddling under the hedges with their greatcoats over their shoulders. It was almost time for them to resume pulling the icy sugar beet tops and they were putting on once more the sodden aprons of old sacks. At that moment the foreman came through the blustery wind carrying a cardboard box. It seemed that, by some dispensation of the Ministry of Food, the gang had earned extra rations because of the overtime it had worked. The foreman spread a sack on the ground and tipped the goods on to it for all to see. There was a two-pound pot of jam, a pound or two of cheese, some tea, sugar, biscuits and tins of egg and milk powder. For one person, perhaps two, it would have made a very acceptable addition to the rations at Christmas but for a dozen it was just an embarrassment. Most of the men began to walk away, too proud to bargain for such paltry offerings. Already they were settling in for another wearisome stretch across the field.

'Don't yer want this heah lovely grub?' the foreman shouted after them. Only the cockney, Bert, remained. A stranger to the reticence of country-bred men, he was keenly interested in the prospect of getting something for nothing. At the last moment Jumbo ambled up, mumbled something about cheese and joined Bert in eyeing the goods avidly. There seemed to be no other serious claimants so the two assumed a personal rivalry for the complete store.

'Toss up,' said Jumbo in a rare triumph of articulation. The foreman had other ideas, seeing the extra rations as a work incentive. 'Tell yew what,' he said, 'the fust one o' yew tew across the fild roight ter the fudder ind, he git the whool lot. Tha's a race, d'ye see? But yew got ter pull an' lay the beet proper fashion. An Bert git 20 yards start cos we know he's allust follerin' on behind. I reckon tha's fair.' He was already striding out the 20 yards from the edge of the field.

Jumbo grunted and clumped to the nearest setting-in point in his great sea boots while Bert placed himself at the 20 yards spot.

'Go' shouted the foreman as they seemed to want some signal to start though it was hardly going to be a sprint and it would be half an hour at least before they reached the far side. He watched them for a few minutes before packing the goods back into the box. The old men of the gang, strung out in an untidy line across the field, took little notice of what was going on for it was not likely to be anything that would ease the ache in their backs. If the foreman was using the parcel of groceries to hasten the work, well, that was his affair, not theirs.

The two men had completed 100 yards of their rows by now

and Jumbo was catching up. He was working steadily and without apparent haste but there was no doubt that he was overhauling rapidly. Bert, on the other hand, was in a frenzy of flailing arms and jerking movements that would certainly sap his energy. Every time he looked back, Jumbo was nearer. With another 200 hundred yards to go to the opposite headland there was no chance but that Jumbo would be there first. The frantic desire to take the goods home to his wife inspired Bert to desperate measures. When Jumbo came level he could not stand the thought of losing and he launched his spare body at the massive Jumbo in a fury. Jumbo staggered for a moment, shook off the futile attack with a single arm movement and after growling something uncomplimentary, went on with his work. In a fever of frustration, Bert stumbled along, the heavy sacking aprons dragging in the mud. For a little while he kept abreast of Jumbo but his city strength could not sustain the effort. While his arms still followed the motions, his legs seemed to give way and he was on his knees and crawling. Then, as if he could do no more, he fell forward on his face. He lay there until the shouts of the old men brought Jumbo stumbling across to haul him up.

The foreman took Bert home, bumping along in the lorry with the box of groceries beside him for at the last moment Jumbo came forward and yielded up the precious prize, his by rights. The gang worked on in the frozen field for another couple of days but Bert did not reappear. As the gang straggled back to the lorry on the last afternoon the foreman looked across to me and waved goodbye and I wondered if he had the same suspicion as I – that guile and a display of histrionics had secured for Bert the goods that he so much desired. But what he and the old men really thought about the matter, no one could tell.

# Nelson and The Volunteers

When, during the last World War, the Home Guard threatened a horrible fate to any invaders rash enough to drop into their particular territory, they were following a tradition of amateur soldiering that is very old indeed. All through the last century the would-be defenders of the realm, or at least their own corner of it, were the Volunteers, as keen as any modern corps and apparently very well turned out. The Victorian Volunteer has been described as wearing a smart, dark blue uniform with white facings on the tunic and a red stripe on the side of the trousers. On duty he wore a Glengarry hat but this could be replaced by a helmet with a formidable spike on ceremonial occasions. He went to camp for two weeks a year and fired a heavy Martin-Henry rifle at an imaginary foe. The fact that neither the Volunteers nor the Home Guard had much chance to show their aggression does not diminish their value or their courage should it have been required.

Earlier than the gallant Volunteers of Victoria's reign, were those who mustered to frustrate Napoleon's threat of invasion. One of the largest and most admired bands of Volunteers at that time in East Anglia was that at Helmingham, where the Earl of Dysart lived and controlled a huge estate. The corps then numbered around 500 men, all armed and clad in uniform at the earl's expense. As colonel of this small army, he drilled and trained it until every man was as smart and efficient as a regular soldier. Most of the Volunteers were of course employees of his lordship or tenants on the estate, which perhaps gives a motive for such a large turn-out but an element of loyalty and esprit de corps was also notably present and this the earl could not have commanded purely by rank and status alone.

On the first anniversary of the formation of the Helmingham corps, the whole body of men assembled and marched to the church. A routine service was in prospect but it turned out to be a much more auspicious day than any could have imagined. Trickling through the villages in the previous few days had come the news of an exciting sea battle at Trafalgar. Since few of the men would have read a newspaper, such information came piecemeal by word of mouth and the details of the conflict were obscure. It was a great opportunity for the Rev Bellman, a great patriot himself, to deliver a sermon which the men would never forget.

He outlined the battle and the great victory over the French and when the Volunteers felt like cheering their heads off, he went on to tell of Nelson's death in action, the bravery of the crew and the country's obligation to look after the families of those whose lives were lost. When the service was over, the men approached their commanding officer, Captain Alefounder (who on this day was deputising for the earl) and asked him to withdraw the amount of one day's pay from every man and apply it to the Patriotic Fund.

Captain Alefounder was most affected by the generous offer and in the fervour of the moment swore that his men were some of the finest in the land and that he would see that they did not lose by their patriotism. He ordered that a shilling should be given to each man present to drink the health of the surviving heroes of Trafalgar.

When the news of the incident came to the ears of the 'Noble Colonel' (the Earl of Dysart), he took pleasure in sharing in the euphoria of victory to the extent of setting aside £50 to be distributed among the men in the way of awards for proficiency.

To ordinary folk, too, the triumph at the battle of Trafalgar and the dramatic death of Admiral Nelson were matters of personal inspiration. There was the Bury shoemaker, Mr Houghton, whose shop was in the Butter Market and who, on the day that he heard the news, went home early to acquaint his wife with the details. The story was told in the *Ipswich Journal* of how Mr Houghton, a sound, healthy man in the prime of life, set out to chop some kindling soon after arriving home. He was not put out to any extent when the chopper slipped and cut his finger though his wife was concerned and told him to come in and she would bind it up.

'Never mind,' he said cheerfully, 'after all, what is a wound like this compared to Lord Nelson's?' He was about to continue the task but faltered, dropped the chopper and fell dead.

# The World of
# John Knowlittle

The remarkable career of 'John Knowlittle', the Norfolk naturalist, began in the most unpromising circumstances in a Yarmouth slum over a century ago. In truth, of course, 'John Knowlittle' was a pseudonym which he adopted when well established in his chosen profession. His real name was Arthur Henry Patterson and he was one of so many at that time who were 'born too soon', that is before the age of educational opportunity, and so were effectively hobbled for the rest of their lives. Yet, could Patterson have done more or left a more convincing legacy if he had the benefit of college or university background instead of the poverty in which he often found himself? Probably it made no difference in the end, for his intense dedication to the study of nature was such as to cancel out all the difficulties.

Life itself was precarious enough when Arthur was born. He was a weak and puny mite looking likely to succumb to the first childish complaint that came along and with the handicap of having to compete with eight brothers and sisters for the little food and care that was available. Yet he alone survived into adulthood of all that unfortunate brood and, though he looked small and bird-like throughout his life, lived in tolerably good health until he was 78. His mother died when he was three and when his father married again his stepmother turned out to be fanatically religious. Outings therefore, in Patterson's childhood, tended to be limited to church and cemetery though he was sometimes allowed to join his father on his allotment. To any other child such places could not have had the slightest appeal but to him they were the sources of wonder and delight. There was so much to see and marvel at in the lowliest offerings of nature.

Whether he received any encouragement at home for this early enthusiasm is very doubtful. At school there was little provision for such matter though the grim teaching of 'the three Rs' was gradually becoming relaxed and a lesson period each week was set aside for 'nature study' and another for 'drawing'. Young Arthur took full advantage of these small concessions and his keen interest was noticed and fostered to some extent by his schoolmaster, William Wallis, who persuaded the boy to continue at school after the age of 14 as a kind of monitor-teacher.

In those years at school, with a good deal of leisure if little money, Arthur laid down the foundations of his future eminence as a Norfolk naturalist through his unswerving love and attention to every form of life that revealed itself about him. Perhaps he was fortunate in one aspect at least in that he was close by and able to spend his time on the Denes and on Breydon water, a particular environment that he took to immediately and which kept him in a constant state of surprise and enchantment. The fish, birds and flowers of the estuary – for he would not specialise in any one form of life – became the boy's Eden.

In 1880, Arthur married Alice Paston, a sweetheart from his childhood and in the years that followed experienced all the hardships of poverty that arose from his lack of skill and education and also from his need to follow at all costs his absorbing work in the field. Torn between his studies and his duty to provide, Patterson moved unhappily from job to job – as tea salesman, insurance agent, temporary postman, theatre usher. Long hours at work meant reduced attention to his observations and more often than not he would get up at three o'clock in the morning to accomplish his own purposes, reaching the Denes or Breydon in early daylight. His only reward at that time was to see the first of his articles on local nature published in the Norfolk press.

Three years after his marriage, Arthur Patterson accepted a job at Preston Zoo at a pound a week. It was a rough initiation into the lives of larger fauna than he had been used to but it enlarged his perspective of the wild and allowed him to make copious notes on his observations. Later they were published under the title *Notes on Pet Monkeys*.

A year later he returned to his old haunts at Yarmouth and was reasonably content with a warehouseman's job at a draper's where he stayed for five and a half years. The long hours within doors and his desire to make closer contact with the natural world caused him to, take another zoo job, this time at Dublin. It was an unhappy experience that left him penniless and unemployed again before working for a few months as a sewing machine agent. Nevertheless, during this period he was busy assembling his written records and during the 1880s several of his books were published – *Seaside Scribblings for Visitors, Notes on Pet Monkeys, A list of the Fish at Great Yarmouth, Broadland Scribblings*. Though there was little monetary reward for any of these, his work earned a prize from the Great Yarmouth Naturalists Society and his name was becoming known to distinguished naturalists all over the country.

It was not until 'John Knowlittle' was 35 years old that he was able to settle down to a tolerably well-ordered and permanent post as school attendance officer. At last he could devote himself to his passionate interest in nature without fear or sense of guilt. Free during the school holidays, he obtained a houseboat and spent happy days meandering among the Broads, his notebook always ready, his curiosity never ceasing. Nothing was ever too minute or too stale – it became important and fresh by his own enthusiasm. He continued to write articles and occasionally give lectures to local societies.

There is no doubt that Patterson saw his role as something more than a student – rather, as a missionary. His urge to disseminate his knowledge to others was almost a divine necessity. 'One feels that not a day goes by but one has

46

managed to let at least one ray of sunshine through at least one person's shutters. Such seems to be the life I have led these years, years that I hope have been of service to others and not unprofitable to myself.'

To be sure, contented years occupied by his favourite way of life mellowed the naturalist as he aged. In an era less sensitive to animal cruelty than we are today he led a call for understanding and sympathy for small wild creatures. His only anger was for 'pseudo-sportsmen' with guns and 'bird-stuffers'.

On his endless excursions along the Broads and on Breydon he was often accompanied by a young protégé named E A Ellis. Ellis had the advantage of belonging to a later generation than Patterson and it was the facility of television that brought that distinguished and well-loved naturalist Ted Ellis into more homes than his mentor had ever achieved with his books.

In 1927 Patterson became vice-president of the Yarmouth Naturalists Society and on May 9th 1935, in the last year of his life, he was honoured to be elected as one of only 25 Associates of the Linnean Society. All the hard work and sacrifices were justified at last.

# Scandal on The Broads

A village activity which has of necessity declined in modern times is that of gossip. Nowadays we have our gossip, like so much else, provided ready-made for us by the media but a few generations ago it was a regular and very powerful element of rural life. After all, what else could country people do? The village was the world reduced to manageable proportions and comprehensible standards. Anything that threatened the set standards, anything less than the most circumspect behaviour according to the local norm could bring the whole weight of village prejudice down on the transgressor's head. A new hat, a strange visitor and a missed church service would be enough to set tongues wagging about some unwary and probably quite innocent neighbour. A disposition to believe the worst of any situation combined with a little imagination have produced some startling tales in the past, none more wildly wrong or more generally believed than that of the Burraway family, who farmed at Martham in the 17th century. And all because of some words on a tombstone.

The village of Martham lies near the Broad of Hickling and the Broad of Martham and is known for its ancient church of St Mary in which, long ago, was placed the memorial that was to cause so much unwise speculation. The inscription read:

'Here lyeth the Body of Christr. Burraway who departed this Life ye 18th. Day of October, Anno Domini 1730 Aged 59 Years. And their lyes Alice, who by her Life was my Sister, my Mistress, my Mother and my Wife. Dyed Feb. ye 12th. 1729. Aged 76 Years.'

As can be seen, the deaths of husband and wife occurred within about 20 months and revealed the woman's age as being about 17 years the older. This fact and the unusual wording of the epitaph aroused the instincts of the local gossips. Was there something improper here? 'Sister, mistress, mother and wife.' It sounded very odd to the suspicious mind. No one seems to have accepted that the words were simply a poetic appreciation of one woman's virtues. Determined scandalmongers constructed a story so involved and credible by its detail that it survived as gospel until very recent years.

The story, nowadays completely discounted, was of the Burraway history and background leading to the final horror of incest and death. In 1671, it was said, young Alice Burraway gave birth to a son following an incestuous relationship with her father, a farmer of Martham. She was only 17, afraid of village condemnation and only too ready to find a solution to the situation by placing the boy, named Christopher, in a distant orphanage. Having declared the child an orphan, Alice had to abandon all rights and claims to the child in the future.

Christopher grew up in the institution and in due course was released to take up employment on a farm. He was a willing worker with an inquiring mind and as he reached manhood he moved from time to time to different farms to better his wages and prospects. The farm that eventually secured his services as a farm steward was that at Martham, now owned by Alice, the elder Burraway having died. Neither Alice nor Christopher had any suspicion of the true relationship between them.

Elevated as he was now to a superior farming position, Christopher had no wish to move further and settled down to work for Alice whom he found to be a fair and reasonable employer. For her part, Alice valued the boy's hard work and responsible attitude on the farm. Seventeen years between them did not hinder a growing dependence on and fondness for each other. It was a natural outcome of their close association that they should agree to marry. For 20 years the couple lived happily together and Alice was an old lady of 75 when the world suddenly turned upside down. Noticing a pattern of moles on her husband's shoulder, she remembered that her baby had an identical arrangement of marks and a hideous suspicion arose in her mind, confirmed when she travelled to the orphanage and was able to examine the records. There was no doubt that Christopher was her own son. The shock to Alice was such as to cause her heart to fail and she died immediately after.

Christopher died in the following year, suddenly losing his strength and purpose, having himself discovered the facts of the relationship after his wife's death. Such is the story that many believed and it fits tolerably well with the information on the memorial tablet and the elegiac 'my Sister, my Mistress, my Mother and my Wife' when interpreted in the basest sense. However, the findings of modern research disprove the theory of incest. Records show that Mr Burraway, Alice's father, was married to a local girl, Mary Lane in October 1671 and their son was a quite legitimate Christopher. The correction does not completely dispel all doubts. Incest between father and daughter could have ceased in 1670, Alice's baby being born in 1671. The second Christopher was born in 1672. Doubts lurk in the mists of long ago together with a wonder that a tragedy of Greek proportions should be played out here in the placid reaches of Broadland.

# Emily's Easter Hat

It was Friday again. Old Emily moved about the kitchen chuckling to herself with pleasure as she prepared Joe's breakfast and watched him eat. She could not be bothered with food this morning. As soon as he had finished she cleared away and washed up and was ready before he had got the pony harnessed to the cart. She had dressed herself in a huddle of old clothes and high, laced boots.

Joe looked at her once as he threw an armful of empty sacks into the cart, muttered something like 'Chris' above' in his beard and took no more notice. He mounted the rickety cart by the round, metal step and sat down heavily on the plank that formed the seat. The pony was restive and Emily waited for it to be still before she ventured to climb clumsily from her side and sit beside Joe. She clutched firmly at the seat as the pony went off at a good pace and jolted her this way and that but it could not stay her pleasure. Only on Fridays was she allowed to go out on the round and on this day it would be out in the country towards Wakes Colne and Earls Colne and perhaps Halstead too, where she had lived as a little girl for five happy years.

After a short journey, during which neither of them spoke, they came up to a row of likely-looking cottages on the edge of a village. Joe shook the reins idly on the pony's rump and eyed the houses closely.

Suddenly he came out with his raucous call: 'Rabbit skins,' he shouted. 'Old rags, rabbit skins, jam jars, old iron!'

Outside the first house, Joe pulled up and silently handed the reins to Emily. 'Old rags' he was shouting as he disappeared round the back of the house. When he came back to the cart with his sack half full, Emily was chuckling to herself.

'There's no need to shout,' she told him, 'not wi' them owd corduroys yew got on. They don't half whistle, Joe. I reckon they c'n hear yew a-comin' a mile away.' Joe said nothing but glowered at the sack and the pony as he went to the back of another house.

Emily chuckled again to herself and settled as comfortably as she could on the hard board. It was a rare nice morning, she thought, nice to be out with him and not cooped up in the cottage now that the spring buds were showing. But he was quick-tempered, was Joe, and she decided that she had better not continue the joke about the corduroys. Enough was enough and it was always enough sooner with Joe than with herself.

A boy of about ten appeared at the gate of one of the cottages. He stood looking, undecided, then came across the road with an apple in his outstretched hand. Emily began to chuckle again. 'He 'on't bite yer,' she said. 'Put yer hand out flat an' he'll take ut. He love a apple.' The boy proffered the apple and the pony took and munched it.

'What's his name?' the boy asked.

'Ain't got no name. Don't need no name,' Emily told him. 'He know well enough when we talk to 'im.' Emily hugged her miscellany of garments comfortably about her and watched the boy return to the gate. Joe came back again, his sack rattling with jam jars and bones and several stiff rabbit skins in his other hand. He threw them into the back of the cart, eyed the collection for a moment, then went off to another house.

A few doors along, a woman stood at the gate holding something that looked like a hat. She came hurriedly across, wearing a pinafore over a stylish dress and self-conscious at being at full view of the neighbours. She was half hiding the hat until she reached the cart, then she reached up and laid it on the seat beside Emily.

'Got no rags,' the young woman said, 'but you can have this hat if its any use. No, I don't want anything for it – glad to get rid of it in a way. I sha'n't ever wear it.'

Emily picked up the hat and was lost in admiration. 'Tha's a really beautiful hat,' she said.

'Well, it was once,' the young woman agreed. 'A lady who bought it in Paris years ago gave it to my mother. Seems a pity but people seem afraid to wear anything showy nowadays – me included.'

The young woman was already retreating across the road, anxious to keep herself to herself. Emily was gazing at the hat, fascinated by the rich, old-fashioned style with its high crown embellished with feathers and the rim awash with tulle. It was the most beautiful thing she had ever been given, she decided. It reminded her of her distant childhood in this very part of Essex and the dreams she had once had of genteel living. Yes, it's genteel, she thought, but more than genteel – it was grand, grander than anything else she possessed.

She lifted the hat on to her head slowly and gracefully, as a great lady would have done all those years ago and felt that she was crowned with glory.

Joe came back to the cart, kicked a few rags into the back, climbed up and took the reins. He threw Emily one glance. 'Chris sake,' he growled, 'take that crazy thing off.' Emily would have taken the hat off gently with proper respect but in a flash of temper he snatched it off and threw it into the back of the cart among the rabbit skins and jam jars. Emily stared at it, then looked ahead, frozen faced.

'That don't look right,' he explained, relenting. They drove along out of the village and took the road towards Colne Engaine and Pebmarsh without another word. The silence made Joe feel guilty and uncomfortable.

'That ain't that it don't look pretty,' he said at last, giving Emily a sidelong glance, 'but that ain't suitable, d'ye see? I reckon people seeing you wearin' that, they'd laugh.'

Emily said nothing. 'Y'see,' Joe went on in a softened voice, 'tha's a hat for special days – when you got special clo's to go with it.'

'Sunday!' Emily brightened suddenly. 'Sunday I could wear it, Joe.'

Joe flicked the reins across the pony's back, thinking that his abiding weakness was saying too much and giving in too easily. Emily was back in good humour. 'That'll be Easter Sunday, Joe.' Joe did not answer. He jumped down again to visit another house. Emily held the reins idly in her hands. After a time she reached back and retrieved the hat from the assorted junk and held it on her knee.

The carriage from the Manor was coming down the road with the pair of smart greys clip-clopping musically on the hard surface and Emily dutifully pulled a rein and brought the cart nearer to the side. Her ladyship was alone in the carriage and was at that moment engaged in poking the coachman with the point of her parasol to persuade him to stop. The carriage halted exactly opposite to Emily and her ladyship now tapped her parasol on the side to secure Emily's attention. Emily was to tell Joe not to forget to call at the Manor. They were spring cleaning and there were piles of things to be taken away. She was anxious to get it all cleared up.

'Very well, Ma'am,' Emily said. 'I'll tell him. He'll come as soon as he can.' In a moment of desperate courage she picked up the hat and showed it in all its glory to her ladyship.

'Tha's a rare beautiful hat, ain't it, ma'am? But he say I ha'n't better wear ut – he say people'd laugh.' Her ladyship had been ready to signal her coachman to drive on but now she stayed to observe the hat and its faded magnificence.

'When I was a little girl,' Emily was saying, forgetting for a moment her lowly station, 'we allust went to church on Easter Sunday in a new bonnet. Somehow that seemed the right time, everything startin' afresh then – primroses an' violets an' birds singin'. But this hat 'on't dew, he say. He say people'd laugh.'

Her ladyship prodded the coachman to bring the hat for her to examine, touched that it seemed a matter of such importance to Emily. For a full minute she inspected the hat closely,

54

turning it this way and that and nodding to herself over some of the colourful details. Then she handed it back.

'Wear your beautiful hat to church on Sunday,' she ordered. 'Your husband is not to stop you coming.'

Joe reappeared as the carriage was pulling away and he touched his forehead with a finger. 'You're to go up to the Manor an' collect the rubbish,' Emily told him, 'an' she say I can wear the hat for chu'ch on Sunday.' Joe drove home in sullen silence.

When Easter Sunday came it was a day effulgent with signs of early spring. Honeysuckle twined its way through hedges beneath which primroses and violets nodded in clusters. Emily was pleased. The church would be decorated this year, just like it used to be and she would be wearing her Easter hat that once adorned the head of some rich Parisian.

Joe gloomily acknowledged defeat. Who was he to oppose the will of two such females? Still, he was unsure that some slight or insult might be done. People could be cruel. 'I reckon I better come tew,' he said gruffly, struggling with collar and unaccustomed tie. Emily spent an age fixing her hair and finally settling the hat in place just like a high-class lady.

The church was almost full when they arrived. Flowers adorned the porch, the pulpit and font and sunlight streamed down on the heads of the congregation. One of the heads turned when Emily and Joe entered, others quickly followed. A hundred eyes now gazed upon the hat. If the gentry had not started to arrive at that moment the more unkind of the congregation would surely have begun to titter. Joe was looking at the floor and waiting for it to happen but Emily kept her head high and her hat grandly visible. Inside, she was counting, a long slow count to the moment when her confidence must break.

Just as the bell stopped tolling, the group from the Manor arrived. The family made its way to the front pew, her ladyship in the lead and the subject of such concerted attention that Emily was momentarily forgotten. On her head was a hat gloriously superior to hats in general, a hat a little more subdued perhaps, but undoubtedly of the same genre as Emily's. For a full minute the congregation gaped, the organ fell silent and Emily felt the tears of sheer relief come to her eyes.

In another week there would be a village fashion for flamboyant hats. Today there were but two and Emily, as she knew, had the finest, the original from Paris, the nonpareil of which others would be but poor imitations. Happily, she gazed around the church as the vicar gave out the number of the hymn. There were primroses and violets bedded in fresh moss about the pulpit and it was like it had been long ago in her childhood and she smiled a little at the memory. Beside her, Joe winked and pulled at his tight collar as they sang together the Easter hymn.

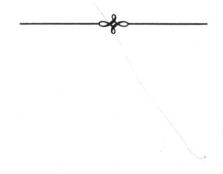

# Samuel Pepys
# At Large

It takes a bit of effort to imagine Samuel Pepys as an East Anglian. Yet his roots were here, his less successful relations still indigenous to Cambridgeshire and the Fens. From time to time Samuel made none too willing journeys into the area and it must be admitted that these forays seldom showed the diarist at his amicable best. A metropolitan by inclination and ambitious to boot, he could find little of pleasure or profit in the countryside. Considering the tribulations of any rural traveller in the 17th century, perhaps his was a commonsense attitude but as it turned out Samuel was constrained to travel a good deal in East Anglia. The farthest expedition that he ever made in this country was to Parson Drove, Wisbech and Chatteris. Cupidity, rather than family affection, was the motive for this adventure into the wilds.

Already, through family circumstances, Samuel had become familiar with the village of Brampton, not far from Huntingdon. It happened that Samuel's uncle, who owned a good-sized house and estate there, died without any immediate family to inherit. All was left, therefore, to his brother, Samuel's father and would pass to Samuel himself on his father's death. It was the sort of good fortune that the diarist, with his eye ever on the growth of his personal wealth, found mightily encouraging. His father was installed in the house at Brampton and on rare occasions Samuel would leave his official duties and important friends and make the tedious journey from London to Cambridgeshire, no doubt eyeing the countryside that he passed through with acute distaste.

Although he must have wished that his relatives and particularly his aged grandfather had lived elsewhere than in the distant Fens, Samuel was all attention again when the possibility arose in 1663 of sharing in another inheritance. His grandfather had married a Wisbech woman named Mary Day whose wealthy father had just died. The hint of a chance of inheriting a slice of the estate excited Samuel's acquisitive sense and he determined to do all he could to secure it even though it would mean a long expedition into the primitive Fens. Another uncle of Samuel together with his son, both named Thomas, also heard the sound of distant music in the demise of old Mr Day and decided to travel to Wisbech at once. Chiefly because of mutual suspicion the two Thomases and Samuel left Brampton together on the first day of the journey. It was to be an eventful one, dogged by mishaps, by bad weather and marshy terrain and made generally miserable by Samuel's complete distrust of his companions who, he feared would take advantage of him if they could.

On 17th September 1663, Samuel complained in his diary: 'With much ado through the fens, along dikes where sometimes we were ready to have our horses sink to the belly, we got by night with great deal of stir and hard riding to Parson Drove – a heathen place.'

No doubt presentday inhabitants of Parson Drove will forgive Samuel's unkind comment. He was cold and tired, having ridden all day and apprehensive of what he believed was a 'miserable inne'. Here at Parson Drove, poor relations of the Pepys family were called on and added to the company, all going to the inn for the night. It was not at all to Samuel's liking. His uncle and aunt Perkins and their daughters were – 'poor wretches, living in a sad, poor thatched cottage, like a poor barne or stable,' and had little in common with Samuel's experience of elegant London life. In great irritation he listened to a young country cousin playing a 'treble' while they waited for supper, then – 'the whole crew (a sad company of which I was ashamed) supped with us.'

After supper there was great excitement when an ostler

announced that one of the horses had been stolen, Samuel taking a grim satisfaction in finding that it was not his. For some reason suspicion was fastened on some poor lawyer's clerk who was staying at the inn and he was secured in his bed while others searched for the horse in the darkness. By midnight, Samuel had had enough of the day's events and retired to bed in a 'sad, cold nasty chamber' only to be awakened again soon after to be told that the horse had been recovered. In the morning he found that he had been 'bit cruelly by the gnatts' and was much put out when he realised that no one else in the party had been bitten by 'gnatts'.

Samuel, with his city manners and his undisguised impatience with nearly everything he met, must have been just as much a trial to his country cousins as they were to him and it was a relief to all when, next day, they came to Wisbech in good time and Samuel recovered some of his urbanity. He liked the town and its association with prominent people of the past and was in good humour when he, with Thomas senior and junior, set off to find Mr Blinkthorne who seems to have been a key figure in the affairs of Mr Day, the deceased.

Mr Blinkthorne was a miller, amiable enough and ready to join the party of fortune seekers for a meal at the inn, where he revealed that he had something to be amiable about. Mr Day's estate had been bequeathed to him and the Pepys family were of little consequence in the matter. Nevertheless, so that they would not go away empty-handed after their long journey he conceded a small portion of the estate. It was enough for the intrepid travellers to set off next morning for Chatteris in right good humour, 'very merry at our defeate.'

# The Great Fire of Debenham

How fortuitous for everyone that Mr Pepys was present, pen in hand, at the Fire of London and the Great Plague. Few of the disasters of the past have been so clearly seen and so well recorded. However, there is a close parallel to Pepys' eyewitness account of the London fire in the story of the Great Fire of Debenham. Admittedly, the witness here was no scribe and it seems probable that he could neither read nor write but there was nothing wrong with his eyesight, his judgments or his long and detailed memory.

His name was David Taylor and he, with other members of the extensive Taylor family, was closely involved in the crushing calamity that visited the village on March 3rd 1744. He was at that time a young lad just starting out to work but it was not until he was a very old man that the stored experiences and observations of the disaster, retained through his lifetime, were set down as the story came from his lips and the account given to posterity in the Dove manuscript. It tells not only the details of the Debenham fire but reveals too, something of how a country village existed in those days.

The fire broke out on the morning of a gusty March day, for the month had come in like a lion and was blowing the dust along the village street. It just happened that David was in the village that morning, something unusual in itself for he was apprenticed to a shoemaker at Framlingham and only occasionally made the journey back to Debenham to see his family and friends. He was about to set off back to Framlingham at about nine o'clock in the morning when he heard a shriek and someone shouting 'Fire'.

The voice David recognised as that of his mother but when he ran back to investigate he found that it was not his mother's house but his grandmother's bakery that was on fire. His grandmother was a widow well known as Rosella Summers who had carried on the bakery single-handed since her husband died.

As David reached the bakery, his brother and his uncle Tom also ran up. They carried ladders and apparently had the intention of getting on to the roof and pulling away some of the thatch but it was a forlorn hope already lost as flames appeared in the thick smoke and began to lick the tinder-dry eaves with a sharp, crackling noise. Rosella stood in the street wringing her hands as a crowd of villagers gathered round her. There was very little that they could do; the stream was some way off and all but dry, and anyway buckets of water would have had little effect on the blaze. A saving piece of fortune was that Rosella's house was on its own, alone on that side of the street. In a short time the bakery, being all dry timber and straw thatch, was no more than a pile of smouldering beams and grey ashes. The villagers watched and sympathised, not knowing that this was but the prelude to a greater tragedy.

As if determined to keep the fire alive, the fresh wind blew sharply on to the smouldering mass, raising showers of sparks as bright as constellations and whirling them high up in the air. It seemed a wonder that they could carry so far, some falling at last in the Friary field, too many dropping on the thatch of the cottages on the opposite side of the street. It took only a few minutes for the whole row of houses to be ignited and fiercely blazing, with the roofs alight first and falling into the interior. Only that one house escaped which had a tiled roof.

Little is mentioned in the account of the fire of the summoning of fire fighters and the part, if any, that they played in the rescue activities. On that first day of the 3rd of March the fire spread in an inferno from house to house all day long. The fires were not put out for two or three days, due chiefly to the difficulty in obtaining water and the conflagration attracted sight-seers from all the villages around, watching in awe as the fire destroyed the village and its inhabitants' livelihoods.

David's father, also a baker, saw his house go up in flames together with ten loads of dry faggots intended for firing the ovens, the whole making a seething mass of flames that added to the sense of wild destruction and annihilation everywhere. David later remembered other people and other incidents in those critical days – the fate of the three journeymen shoemakers, for example, who lived together in a tenement and were not seen again after the fire. There was also the Quaker John Long, also a shoemaker, who survived the blaze but lost his house and business. Determined not to be beaten by the catastrophe, John Long later set out to build another house with his own hands but had not the health or strength to finish it. He found it impossible to get into the shoemaking business again without any premises and he died a few years later in the workhouse.

David recalled a little cobblers' stall that stood against the wall of one of the houses and which, amid all the desolation around, was somehow saved as men with long cromes pulled it away from the house. Four shoemakers had worked in that small space and they were no doubt gratified to think that they could carry on with their business – if ever there was work again for them to do.

As March 4th developed into another fine, windy day, the fire continued to spread since little practical help had arrived to quench the flames. Good intentions came from the farmers of Winston, Pettaugh and Framsden who were concerned enough to send men with teams of horses with the idea of pulling down the thatch of houses at risk. Unfortunately, they made the same mistake that Pepys had noted in the Fire of London – the rescuers were following the fire instead of going ahead of it. People who had earlier grabbed buckets from the church continued to carry small quantities of water from the stream but might have saved themselves the trouble for all the good that it did. On the third day the fire died down simply from lack of more properties to consume. Altogether 33 houses were burnt to the ground including every one standing along the road from the corner by the river to Girling's meadows. The devastation of the village and of people's lives was cruelly complete.

Survivors and neighbouring villages gave what help they could to stricken Debenham with practical assistance and with pathetically small collections of money. David's father clearly saw the impotence of the village against such catastrophes in the future unless there was proper organisation and preparedness and he generously opened a subscription with the aim of buying a fire engine. It was a dream as yet too distant to realise. What cash there was to spare was needed for immediate succour and rebuilding of homes. In a short time it became obvious that the amount needed to buy a fire engine would never be reached. The best that the people of Debenham could do against any future catastrophe was to pray.

# The Strong Men

Victor Hugo's ex-convict hero Jean Valjean was alone able to lift a waggon from an injured man and through this feat of strength gave away his identity to the watching gendarme. With less to lose, John Punchard of Bedfield, who was a notable strong man of the last century, accomplished almost exactly the same task. A primitive style of threshing machine had broken down and stood lop-sided in the mud without its large fourth wheel. It was the sort of casualty that had happened before and generally required three muscular farm hands to lift the corner of the machine while two others manhandled the wheel on to the axle. John was not trying to prove anything as did some strong men with more flamboyant natures and if he could have called on others to help he would have done so. As it was, the job had to be done. He put his shoulder under the corner and used his immense strength to lift. The wheel was put on and John's achievement acclaimed among the humble devotees of such giants.

In our own time the necessity for lifting heavy weights has been taken literally out of our hands. The fork lift, the elevator, the power hoist and such aids have released countrymen from the centuries-old practice of carrying heavy burdens on their backs but in the farming past it was a necessary and important side of daily work. Those men who were particularly muscular were proud of their strength and usually the top men on their farms. Nowadays we are inclined to jib at any weight of more than half a hundredweight (56 pounds) but a few decades ago such a finicking amount would have earned the farmer's contempt since he expected potatoes to be in hundredweights and corn to be carried in 12 stone sacks.

John Punchard's modesty confined his feats of strength to

64

the daily requirements of farm work and he had no patience with public shows and demonstrations of power. Even if he had such ambitions, he would have been quickly reduced to size by his sensible and forthright wife who regarded him with a mixture of pride and derision. Lifting heavy loads, she told him, was something any donkey could do. At the same time, it was well known among the farm men that she fed him great helpings of the best food to keep his muscles in trim.

However, there were some who saw a distinct challenge in John's weightlifting capabilities. Ted Whiteman, head man at Pond Farm not two miles distant, soon made it widely known that he was prepared to outlift John any day. Arno Martin from Debenham thought so too. Surprisingly, Arno was not a farm man at all but a postman whose prowess was whispered far and wide. It was believed that he could carry a quarter of a ton of planks of wood on his shoulders and could pitch a full sack of oats into a waggon with a fork. No one else had ever been known to do this and it was regarded with almost as much awe as his capacity for drinking large quantities of gin and water.

Even more renowned was Sid Crowe who, on a well-witnessed occasion carried two sacks of flour and a coomb of wheat three times around the farmyard. He was invited to finish the performance by stepping over a broomstick held a few inches from the ground but this obstacle defeated him and he never tried this particular trick again. There was talk of another farm man who could carry two coombs of corn, one under each arm and not only walk with them but also mount a short ladder to load the sacks into a waggon. He could also hold two 56 pound weights in one hand above his head. From a village near Saxmundham came news of another Samson whose particular achievement was to clasp a sack of corn in his arms and lean backwards until his head almost touched the ground. He could then straighten up again without losing either the sack or his balance.

There were many people, especially among the ordinary

level of farm workers who marvelled at such accomplishments, who believed that there should be proper, supervised trials of strength between the giants. The giants themselves had little enthusiasm for the idea, partly because each man's achievement was peculiar to himself, something he had perfected to his own satisfaction and could not be regarded as part of a general contest. Besides, while each strong man was an undisputed king in his own farmyard, a competition with others could result in a loss of prestige if he were not the winner. So far as is known, the strong men of the farms never met in a formal contest but chose to nurture their reputations among their own followers.

Anyway, it was something that the men's wives found little virtue in since it earned them nothing extra. As Mrs John Punchard remarked on the Sunday morning following John's feat with the thresher: 'You being so good at lifting things, 'haps you can manage to lift that there prayer book an' come along o' me to church.'

# A Shilling For A Wife

Robert Whiting was a Sudbury weaver at a time when the town was still noted for its craft. He was a simple man, given to such modest pleasures as fishing in the Stour of a Sunday morning and sometimes walking to the Long Melford Bull on a Saturday night. There was no time for anything else. Long hours at the loom and dedication to his work kept Robert rather shy and reserved and single. He was glad to have a good friend in his neighbour Henry Frost to whom he found he could confide himself.

It was in the course of one of his conversations with Henry during the spring of 1821 that he confessed that he wished he was married and that he possessed such a neat, capable wife as Henry's. Mrs Frost, it was clear, was greatly admired by Robert. She was no beauty, he admitted to himself but perhaps all the better for that. She was tidy and clean yet seemed often to arouse her husband's irritation by her quiet demeanour. It was something that Robert found difficult to understand and he could only feel a deep envy of his friend. Whenever Robert visited their house he made no secret of his admiration and caused Henry to begin to think shrewdly about a possible bargain for all three. It was one day in May when he took Robert aside and told him that he was prepared to sell him his wife.

The honest weaver was so shocked that he made no answer that day. He had heard of such things, with the wife being led out of the house with a halter around her neck according to tradition and exchanged for a token sum of money but he believed that it had only happened years ago. Henry reassured him by recounting the story of Sam Balls of Blythburgh who had recently sold his wife. Sam had apparently been a fairly jovial character but found that his boisterous behaviour and shrewish wife did not mix well together. Sam had drawn up a proper legal document that was witnessed and signed by no less authority than the village constable himself. He then proceeded to hand over his wife to his neighbour Abraham Rede for a shilling. It was all true, vowed Henry but omitted to mention to the ingenuous Robert that the transaction had taken place nearly 30 years before.

Robert was deeply impressed by the story and even more by the account of a farmer at Stowupland who had sold his wife to a neighbour for five guineas. The high price suggested some hard bargaining and the farmer was reported to be so pleased at the exchange that he presented his departing wife with a guinea to buy a new gown.

Nevertheless, both Robert and Henry were aware that there was a growing antagonism to such arrangements, particularly by women who decried such degradation to their sex. The instances of wife selling that they knew about had all taken place in tucked away villages – could it be accepted so readily in a town like Sudbury? After all, it was 1821 and there was a great movement towards more modern ideas. It seemed a bit like asking for trouble. However, after more discussion the two men and presumably the woman resolved to go ahead. The nominal sum agreed was one shilling and six pence and the procedure to be followed was the accepted formality of Henry leading his wife out of the house with a halter around her neck while Robert stood by to receive her.

Unfortunately for Robert, it was not to be. Already there was a crowd of women in the street, outraged and hostile, giving no doubt that they were intent on drastic physical revenge for such scandalous behaviour. The would-be bridegroom took in the picture of shaking fists and furious faces and could think of no more suitable action at the moment than to take to his heels at the highest speed possible. With a feminine discrimination whose logic escaped him, Robert found the whole mob of angry females behind him while Henry was escaping Scot free. Robert seemed to be facing a fate as least as bad as death and in desperation he scurried up somebody's garden path and into the open door of a cottage. There, he found that nothing so slight as a door was likely to stay the horde of implacable females for they were pounding on it in the next moment. Rushing past the astonished old couple in the parlour, he could see no means of immediate exit by another door and so went flying up the stairs. Here, there was no hiding place except a small room at the back where he stayed in growing panic until the mob below burst open the street door and swept up the stairs. The only escape now for the weaver was to take his life in his hands and jump out of the window. Fortunately the garden below was well-tilled and soft and Robert found himself not much the worse for the fall. As he applied his full energies to the task of vaulting a series of garden fences and putting as much space as possible between himself and the shrill sounds of the man-hunt, he surely learned that the public conscience had moved on since the days when wife selling was tolerated.

Similar public – and largely feminine – demonstrations of opinion against other people's domestic morals were used with frightening effect on some occasions. One of these took place outside the house of a tradesman of Bury St Edmunds, who was believed to be cruel to his wife. In fact, it was his third wife and the general conclusion was that he had been equally, and perhaps fatally, unkind to all of them. He was known to be surly and bad-tempered and had roused the ire of his neighbours because of his grouchy behaviour. This spontaneous demonstration of public anger came when it was heard that by some further bad treatment of his wife, she had run away. Some 400 people gathered and set up such a threatening clamour in front of his house that the man was in fear for his life. The crowd pounded on the door and tried all means of getting into the house but found all bolted and barred. Frustrated, some of the mob made a rough effigy of the man, hung it on the door and gave it a hundred lashes of a cat o' nine tails. Somehow the quarry escaped from the house and threw himself on the protection of the law. In due course, a posse of constables arrived in company with the full authority of an Alderman and the crowd dispersed.

Punishment by public censure was obviously effective in the days when law men were few and it was regularly used in the treatment of local misdemeanours by the setting up of stocks on market day or by the pillory. A period of a few hours in either of these shaming devices invited both judgment and castigation from the passers-by. If the crime was serious or touched on the sensitive areas of the public conscience there could be violent anger vented in vicious attacks on the pilloried one.

One Saturday a schoolmaster was placed in the pillory at Ipswich for the attempted rape of three girls. He was soon surrounded by an indignant crowd and pelted so severely with missiles that he had to be taken down, unconscious and seriously ill. If the officers had not intervened at that moment he would certainly have been killed.

# The 'Royal'
# at Bury St Edmunds

According to my calculations, it would have been my great grandfather who had the privilege of attending what was probably the greatest agricultural event in East Anglia during the last century – the Royal Show at Bury St Edmunds. Being a farmer himself, he would have made sure he was one of that multitude that filled the lanes each day for a week in that July of 1867 to follow the crush to the show ground. Yes, great grandfather would not have missed that event no matter what the difficulties and nor would all the 33,000 others who managed to do so and most of them on shank's pony. The excitement at that time, because of the revolutionary changes that had taken place on farms since the last Royal Show, was immense and the lasting wonder never diminished. The vast amount of machinery was almost beyond belief, perhaps for the first time of more interest than livestock. Traction engines that were incredibly mobile over the show ground and ploughs and cultivators powered by steam at static demonstrations were but the beginning of the new attractions.

Long before, the little town had been caught up in a fury of preparation by all the inhabitants. Enterprise may not formerly have been the main virtue of the locals but the show became a torch to light up ideas, not least those which had to answer the problems of accommodation and feeding for the expected multitude. To be sure, farmers and the better off would come on horseback or make up family parties in carts, waggons and other vehicles but many would never be able to make the journey home on foot after the show was closed. In fact the town was swamped, every street a flowing tide of humanity beneath the flag-decked upper windows. Every house seemed to be able to find spare rooms or accommodation of some kind, while other homes made the strange and sudden transformation into cafes and restaurants. Day and night there was activity of the liveliest kind. One imaginative tobacconist on the Angel Hill placed a small flame in a lantern with a supply of spills at the side and a notice inviting passers-by to use them. As the crowds passed down Angel Hill in the evening, not yet replete with excitement, they would crowd into the Abbey Gardens where a fete was in progress.

The 'Royal' was undoubtedly the best it had ever been, 42 acres in extent and lying beside the railway line to Haughley, a site cleverly chosen for its picturesque charm as well as its convenience. The whole area, but particularly in Market Street and Abbeygate Street, was festive with flags and the gayest of decorations. How heavy hearted was everyone on the first day with the weather cold and wet and the only good news being the arrival of HH the Viceroy of Egypt who promptly bought 40 steam cultivators and went away again. For the rest of the week the weather was everything that could be desired.

Visitors to the show passed directly into the machinery compound and were inclined to spend most of their time there. All the famous names – Ransomes and Sims, Turners, Garretts, Burrell – were showing off the achievements of their traction engines and static steam engines. One traction engine, to the considerable wonder of the spectators, was so manoeuvrable that its steering wheel was fixed to allow it to go round in endless circles without a driver.

Great progress was shown in the use of steam for cultivation. Trials by the Royal Agricultural Society had already been made in connection with steam engines, fixed and portable, for threshing, chaff-cutting, mills, oil-cake breakers and the like. Now, at the show itself there were fixed demonstrations of ploughing and cultivating, with two 14 horsepower machines fitted with windlass drums to draw two ploughs – or cultivators – from side to side of a field simultaneously.

Everywhere astonishment was expressed at the widespread use of iron in implements. A kind of disbelief attended the remarks of many of the bystanders – that there were ploughs of which only the handles were made of wood, that there were no longer any land rollers or frames of machines or toothed wheels except those that were made of metal. Most surprising, according to general opinion, was the common use of iron field gates and posts. Such things were not easily absorbed by traditionalists and one writer at least found he appearance of so much iron had 'an oddness very striking to the unpractised eye.'

Obviously one of the real miracles achieved by the modern machinery was in hay-making. A machine to toss the hay could do the work of a score of men and women with pitch forks. Just to watch the efficient way that it whirled the hay about and allowed it to settle gently in orderly rows was to realise what great steps modern farming methods were making.

Important though the farm animals were at the show, with the horses of particularly keen interest, it is the show's importance as a mark of the evolution of agricultural ingenuity in machinery that provides the greater interest in looking back. Great strides were being taken at that time.

On the last day of the show, when the admission price was reduced to a shilling, half the world seemed to turn up at Bury, by every means possible. A concourse began in the early morning, with waggons and carts so dense that they formed endless processions along all the incoming roads. Very soon they had filled up every yard and enclosure and still blocked the streets which had also filled up with pedestrians from the trains. Yet in the end somehow the local families coped and won by determined hospitality. Whatever else was accomplished at the Bury Show it was a triumph of goodwill.

# The Stansfield Murders

Murder is no respecter of persons or of wealth. It was a Norfolk mansion that witnessed one of the most shattering crimes of the times, perpetrated in the very centre of rural peace. It was so tranquil for the potential victim that he smoked his cigar after dinner that evening with a sense of contentment. His usual routine was to walk to the outer door to take in some fresh air before going to bed. In seconds he was dead, shot in the heart at a range which made certain of the target. Hearing the shot, a younger man hurried to investigate and was also shot and killed. There remained two women and in turn each was shot and wounded. In a few minutes servants were in hysterics and calling on farming neighbours for help in the limitations of the days when communications were difficult in rural areas.

The two men killed were father and son, Mr Isaac Jermy and Mr Jermy Jnr. The Jermys lived at Stansfield Hall, near Wymondham, a considerable edifice. At one time the family name was Preston but because of a substantial bequest, including Stansfield Hall, it was readily agreed to take the name of the benefactor. At the same time Mr Isaac Jermy became one of the most prominent figures in the county, as a magistrate, a chairman at Quarter Sessions and Recorder at Norwich.

With extensive landed wealth, Mr Jermy held several farms which were tenanted by working farmers. One of the principal tenants was Mr James Rush, who lived in some style at Potash Farm. In addition he was tenant of two other farms including the home farm of Stansfield Hall so that initially there must have been fairly close agreement between the two. Very soon, however, the landlord began to feel some disquietude as to the farm management and even more alarmingly as to the increasing debts and the general squandering of money. As much as £3,753 was owed to the estate on a mortgage and little done to reduce it. In October 1847, Mr Jermy felt compelled to curb the debts and among other measures restricting James Rush's prodigality, decided to eject him from his superior Potash Farm to a cottage on the estate, an obviously humiliating experience. In the following year, the landlord brought an action in law against Rush on a breach of covenant. The farmer was by now consumed by resentment and the desire for revenge.

Was Rush indeed the murderer? The crime was committed on the 28th November 1848, and from the first the suspicion fell full on him despite his precautions at sowing a false trail. Gradually, after the total horror of the family's massacre, the public learned of the devious preparations and the inevitable steps that led to a conviction.

Part of the calculation was the employment of a young woman as a governess for his children. Emily Sandford quickly became enmeshed in evil plots and when the farmer became Emily's lover, she was ready to agree to anything that he suggested. To begin with, she was required to prepare a series of forged documents purporting to make a legal claim to the whole of the Stansfield Hall estate. The papers were hidden under the floorboards in a bedroom, awaiting a profitable time to use them. They were discovered at the police search.

Also brought to the light of day were the articles of woman's clothing which Rush used as a disguise. At about eight o'clock on the evening of the 28th, he donned a dress and an old-fashioned bonnet that carefully shielded his features, then wrapped himself in a voluminous cloak. Under the cloak he carried a double-barrelled gun. In the darkness his shifty movements and queer apparel attracted no one's attention on the short distance to the mansion. Very soon he was hidden in the shrubbery close by the door.

James Rush knew well enough the routine of the Jermy family in autumn evenings. There would be a leisurely dinner in the dining room for the Recorder and his son and daughter-in-law, often followed by tea partaken in comfort in the drawing room. The younger couple would then attend to the children's bedtime in another part of the house. On this fateful night, Mr Jermy kept to his habit of taking a breath of fresh air before bed and accordingly moved to the open door of the porch. He could not have believed that his existence would be extinguished suddenly by a grotesque figure in the shrubbery with his gun already loaded and cocked.

Almost at the same instant that he took in the weird sight, he received the shot close up in the region of the heart. In a few seconds he was dead. Rush then entered the house holding the gun and when the son hurried to the drawing room to discover why a shot had been fired, he was immediately confronted by the murderer. The two men had found themselves so close there was scarcely room to lift the gun. There was an explosion that crashed through the rooms while the younger Jermy silently crumpled and fell in the doorway, his life already extinct.

Not satisfied with such carnage, Rush then stalked through the rooms and eventually found Mrs Jermy Jnr and a servant, Eliza Chastney in the hall. For one reason or another his marksmanship was faulty. Without hesitation, he raised his gun and fired twice but perhaps because of some remaining dregs of humanity succeeded in only wounding the women. Mrs Jermy Jnr was shot in the arm, Eliza in the leg.

By this time the domestic staff were shattered and panic-stricken, their once-peaceful domicile torn apart by tragedy. As soon as they could move in safety the two wounded women were nursed and the young children taken swiftly to the comparative refuge of the coach house. The butler ran for help to nearby farmhouses and a hurried journey was made to Wymondham from where it was possible to send a message by telegraph to Norwich police.

When the extent of the gory havoc was revealed to the police there was an immediate move to surround farmer Rush's house. Despite his disguise, certain of the servants had recognised him as he fled out of the door. There was no escape. Rush spent the last night in his cottage in a state of craven fear. Having spent his hate against the Jermy family there seemed to be nothing left but guilt, so cowardly that he was reduced to begging for support from Emily Sandford, who promised to provide an alibi. It made no difference – evidence of guilt was overwhelming and the alibi was too flimsy to stand.

Rush was brought before the magistrates at Wymondham and later tried at the Norwich Shirehall, electing to defend himself for the six days of the hearing. In March 1849, he was executed on Castle Hill before an immense crowd curious to see what manner of man could have committed such a dastardly crime.

# Ned Painter
# Norfolk's Champion

Well, what happened to Ned Painter in the end, then? No one knows, nor what happened to him in the beginning, come to that. But we do know quite a lot about the middle years and that was exciting enough for a whole lifetime.

Ned Painter, that true son of bygone Norfolk, whose massive frame and flattened nose evoked the hero worship of thousands, had the physique and the stamina that made him one of the great prize fighters of the early 19th century. His name earned mention beside the immortals like Tom Cribb and Tom Belcher and those of the sporting fraternity who could walk or ride or merely limp or crawl would somehow get to the venue of a fight to watch such giants in combat. At that time there was an almost hysterical excitement attached to the sport.

They were proud days for Norfolk's followers of the noble art when Ned arrived from obscurity and soundly defeated Coyne and, soon after, Alexander. On December 16th 1817, Ned met the formidable Sambo Sutton on Bungay Common. It was his first great fight at national standard. An immense crowd invaded the common, with county gentry and yokels for once equal in their enthusiasm. It was reported in the *Norfolk Chronicle* afterwards that there were also 'several well-dressed women' who, with every one else, saw Sutton roundly beaten in 15 rounds.

After the fight Ned announced, to the consternation of everyone, that he would not fight again. It was an incredible decision. With only successes behind him and a promising career ahead it seemed a tragic waste of talent to give it up. No one could guess the agonies of considered pros and cons that had brought him to this decision. A handful of people knew the truth.

The fact was that Ned had fallen in love with a pretty Norwich girl and was determined to marry her. Unfortunately, she belonged to a family of Quakers of the most rigid beliefs. There would be no consent to the marriage while Ned continued as a prize fighter. On the other hand, if Ned gave it up the father would gladly endow the union with his blessing and also provide for Ned's future by installing him as the host of a respectable inn where he could entertain his friends and live in comfort.

It was common sense to accept such an offer, whatever Ned felt at the halt to his ambitions. The wedding preparations were begun and negotiations set in hand to acquire the inn. Then, out of the world that Ned thought he had left behind suddenly came Tom Spring with a list of successes to his name and a direct challenge to Ned. He was backed by a fight-hungry populace eager to get Painter into the game again. So much pressure made Ned consider the possibility of one more fight, promising the Quaker family that this would really be his last bout. On these terms the girl agreed to wait and Ned gave his attention to training and preparation.

On April 1st 1818, the fight took place at Mickleham Downs before a crowd estimated at 20,000 and with Tom Cribb and Tom Belcher acting as seconds. According to past form Painter was bound to be an easy winner and there was heavy betting on this result but as round followed round in this brutal, bare-fisted contest, it became obvious that he was taking most of the punishment and was in a very groggy state. Sheer courage kept Ned on his feet until the 31st round, when he was finally down and out. Many of the punters were audibly unhappy with the result.

So far as Ned was concerned, this was definitely his last fight. He had been fairly beaten and it was time to attend to the forthcoming wedding and the prospect of following the comparatively uneventful life of an inn keeper.

Fate crept in again, however. Two newspapers of the more sensational kind came out with an implication that the bout with Spring had been fixed. The suggestion was scurrilous, beneath contempt, for everyone in the game who mattered knew Ned to be completely honest.

But the mud had been thrown. Furious with indignation at this slur on his fighting record, Ned decided that the only decisive way to clear his name was to fight Spring again. There would be no prize money and no backers, a straightforward contest without strings of any sort. Once more, Ned had to reject the prospect of domestic bliss and instead set up a series of sparring exhibitions in Norwich, much to the disgust of the Quaker family. His dedicated training was rewarded when the fight took place on August 7th 1818. In front of the vast crowd the bout lasted for 42 rounds, with Ned the eventual victor.

Satisfied that he had vindicated his honour, Ned once more declared that he would never fight again and returned to Norwich. In due course he was forgiven by his Quaker bride-to-be and, still grudgingly, by her father. Soon after, the young couple were married and on January 1st 1820, it was announced that Ned was about to take over the Sun and Anchor tavern in Lobster Lane and would give private lessons in sparring.

This should have been the perfect happy ending to the story but in fact Ned participated once more in one of the great fights of that century against the renowned Tom Oliver. The account of this famous contest is immortalised in the pages of George Borrow's *Lavengro*. What it was that brought Ned back from his comfortable life to the violence of bare-fisted fighting and how strongly his young wife and father-in-law must have protested at the idea can only be guessed at. Whatever the motive, the notion of a bout between Ned and Tom Oliver sent the sporting world into a clamour of excitement.

On Monday, July 17th 1820, in a field near North Walsham, described by Borrow as being 'in the precincts of the old town, near the field of the chapel', the pugilists met. Remote as the venue must have proved for many, something like 20,000 dedicated followers of the sport found their way to the spot, a substantial number from London, others from distant shires. A platform had been rigged up and 60 waggons were drawn up in a circle all round the makeshift ring for the convenience of spectators. Tom Oliver was seconded by Belcher and Cribb and Painter by Tom Spring, now his close friend.

The fight was over in twelve rounds, a popular triumph for Ned who was carried victoriously into North Walsham in a flag-bedecked waggon. That evening the celebrations continued with a dinner attended by all the notables of the sporting world and with Ned as honoured guest. On the following Saturday a benefit night was held at the Swan Inn in Norwich where Ned once more assured his listeners that he had fought his last fight.

This time it was true. There is no record of Ned fighting again or indeed anything about him at all. The *Norfolk Chronicle* no longer found him newsworthy and he was allowed to continue his life in peace.

# A 'Nine Daies Wonder' to Norwich

A highway much used in the past was the road from London to Norwich, a city once no doubt considered remote and something of an adventure to reach. On foot or on horseback or by various kinds of conveyances as they were developed, the journey was made through tedious hours and lonely stretches of road by people to whom travel was never synonymous with comfort. Perhaps the strangest individual to use that road was Will Kemp, on his much-publicised 'nine daies wonder', in which he set out to dance every step of the way and achieve one of the minor adventures of the age of Elizabeth.

Will was a fool in the Shakespearean sense, a clown of consummate art at his best but of a vast egotism on the stage and a tendency to overdo his part. His immediate disadvantage was that his predecessor was the renowned Dick Tarlton, in whose shadow Will was destined to languish, some said with resentment. Certainly a feeling of insecurity, of waning popularity, seemed to haunt the man. Nevertheless, he was frequently called on by Shakespeare's company of players to perform the comic parts – Launce and Dogberry, Justice Shallow, Touchstone and Launcelot and the grave digger in Hamlet, which was always in danger of being wrecked by Will's jokes and asides. His inability to stop embellishing the lines and showing off to the groundlings earned reproof from the master-playwright himself. 'Speak no more than is set down,' Shakespeare admonished, but Will was incorrigible. Besides inserting his own witticisms into the plays he would always give a little jig at the end of the performance.

Ever hankering after popular esteem, Will could not avoid the truth that comparisons made between him and the ghostly Tarlton were seldom to his advantage. He feared that his star was waning. He needed a boost, a fantastic achievement that would be his alone, something that would bring the great and the humble through the breadth of the land to acclaim his virtuosity. If the public could not or would not come to London to see Will Kemp, then he would take Will Kemp to the public.

On the 2nd of February, 1599, Will set out from London dressed as a morris dancer and with a taborer in attendance to proclaim his arrival at towns and villages along the way. The quixotic venture was already well known and as he danced through Whitechapel, Bow and Stratford he was cheered on his way and given a particularly rousing reception at Ilford. However, being in good time and it being a fine, moonlit night he pushed on to Romford for his first night's stay. The target on the second day was Brentwood but again encouraged by 'the moone shining brightly, I tripped to Ingatestone'.

A little further along the road – 'a number of County People and many Gentlemen and Gentlewomen were gathered to see me, Sir Thomas Mildmay standing at his Parke gate received kindly a payre of garters of me (gloves, points and garters being my ordinary merchandize.)'

Will spent the third night at Chelmsford and from there danced to Braintree, Sudbury and Long Melford. At Sudbury he was joined by a young butcher who quickly tired and was treated with scorn by a 'lusty countrie lassie' who took his place and danced with Will, much to his delight, all the way to Melford where she left with a 'courtesie'.

Then to Bury St Edmunds by way of Clare, where Kemp 'rested at the house of a bountiful widdow'. Arrival at the town gate of Bury was an occasion for the largest and most delirious reception of any that he had yet encountered. Considering that this was early February, icy or wet and muddy underfoot on the rough-surfaced roads, the progress of the clown in the short hours of daylight had been phenomenal and country people turned out to show their admiration.

The dancer enjoyed his stay at Bury and perhaps it was there, having been delayed by a heavy fall of snow, that he wrote and dedicated a description of his Nine Daies Wonder to a lady of Elizabeth's court, Mary Fitton, 'a mayde of Honour to the most Sacred Mayde, Royall Queene Elizabeth'. It was believed by many that Mary Fitton was the Dark Lady of Shakespeare's sonnets.

However, even with the acclamation of the crowd ringing in his ears, Will would stay not a minute longer than his schedule required and on a clear, still morning with snow not deep enough to hinder, he was off to Thetford in the dark at seven o'clock and in three hours was at his destination.

When Norwich eventually came in sight, he 'perceived so great a multitude' waiting to greet him that he was constrained by his instinct to make the most of a special occasion, to borrow a horse and ride into the city in triumph. There were crowds on each side of the street and waits accompanied his progress with viol, violin and with singing. An almost royal reception followed, with the Lord Mayor bestowing on Kemp the style and title of 'Freeman of Merchant Adventurers and King of English Morris dancing for ever'.

While in Norwich, Will must have been dancing still, for he recorded this incident in his journal:

'Passing by the Market Place, it was the mischaunce of a homely mayde in long petticoats tyde with points to come unluckily in my way as I was fetching a leape and it fell out that I sett my foote in her skirts; the point either braking or stretching – offfell her petticoat from her waste. The poore wench was so ashamed . . .'

The whole story of Will Kemp's strange journey, with some imaginative additions, has been told in a long, romantic ballad by Alfred Noyes. There was little hint of romance in Will's own account though he was certainly keenly interested in the fair sex and obviously immensely cheered by the admiration of rosy-cheeked country girls. But a Norfolk milk-maid was not the prize he sought. His ego needed the adulation of crowds and he was prepared to suffer considerable discomfort to earn it. The enterprise, bizarre as it was, had been a success for all. It had brought a touch of gaiety to quiet roads and a hint of London's excitement to dull lives in the country while Will had proved that he could captivate the public outside the theatre. London would welcome him back and he would be remembered.

But in his wildest expectations, the fool could never have imagined that we would still be talking of him now, nearly 400 years later.

# The Miracle of St Osyth

Legends are stories which we usually find rather hard to swallow. The sense of improbability irks our common sense and we are inclined to be disparaging of tales which cannot be verified. Yet most legends have a basis in fact and only the subsequent superstitious embellishments cloud the reality. Such is the case with one of East Anglia's most notable legendary figures, St Osyth.

Osyth was of royal birth and a martyr in the cause of Christianity in its earliest days in Britain. She was later proclaimed a saint for her virtuous life and unswerving courage and perhaps also because of the apparent miracles that followed her death. The fascination of the superstitious for headlessness – headless horses, headless riders, headless ghosts – emerges in her story. But it is at such points, when our patience tends to balk, that perhaps we should try and separate the real from the fantastic. There is something of both in this legend, with plenty of reality mainly due to the number of associations that have survived. The village of St Osyth itself, looking across the lonely marshes to the Colne estuary, keeps the story alive in its references to the saint and nearby the name of Nun's Wood indicates the spot where Osyth was slain.

Osyth was the daughter of King Frithewald and Queen Wilburga, a princess of independent spirit from her earliest childhood. In this tiny kingdom of over 1,300 years ago she quickly showed her readiness to learn and equally to speak her mind. Impressed, the king placed her in the care and tutelage of Modwen, a Saxon saint and from him Osyth received the spiritual guidance and encouragement that was to shape her life.

86

Quite early on she accepted the Christian ethic of one god above all and as she grew older she used her influence as a royal princess to set about denouncing the gods and superstitions of old. Seeing the troubles that would ensue from such interference with ancient beliefs, the king and queen called upon her to desist and to consider the normal destiny of one in her station – marriage to an appropriate suitor. For answer, Osyth vowed that she would be a virgin and a nun. It was a frustrating situation for the royal parents who had already picked out as eminently suitable as bridegroom the dashing young Sighere, King of Essex. In the end, they decided that tradition and their royal wishes must take precedence over their daughter's advanced ideas and decreed that she would marry Sighere forthwith, like it or not.

Osyth, however unwilling, felt bound to obey the command but passed the days before the wedding in a dedicated routine of spiritual contemplation and in prayers that she might escape the fate so odious to her. At the appointed day a great wedding feast took place with the compliant Osyth sitting beside the lusty young king. In the midst of the noisy celebrations, a messenger arrived and told the king that a stag of great size and beauty had been seen nearby. Immediately, Sighere excused himself from the table and called for horse and hunting spear. As it turned out, the stag was both swift and cunning and led the royal party far away into the country-side. The king was absent on the hunt for three days.

Perhaps this was one of the miracles that seem to have accompanied Osyth throughout her life and after. Certainly she took the situation as heaven-sent and while Sighere was away took sacred vows as a nun before hastily summoned bishops and then straightway donned the habit. When Sighere returned from hunting the stag, he found that a more precious quarry had escaped him. With truly kingly tolerance he forgave Osyth and presented her with the village of Chiche, complete with nunnery. No longer subject to worldly dictates, the princess now applied herself to religious works including the building of a church dedicated to St Peter and St Paul. She loved the calm beauty of Chiche and the countryside around and was content.

Suddenly, violence and horror arrived in this sleepy corner of Essex when, in October 653, a mob of Danes led by Inguar and Hubba descended on the village. Searching for loot, the Danes sacked the nunnery, in the process murdering many of the nuns. Because of her obvious authority, Osyth was brought forward to confront the Danish chief who offered to spare her life if she would renounce Christianity. There was only one answer that Osyth could make and that in the clear, certain voice of her faith. At a spot in Nun's Wood later identified as being the source of a stream, she was beheaded.

So much of Osyth's story is credible – much of what comes after is touched with superstition. We are told that, headless, Osyth carefully picked up her head and carried it for half a mile to the church of St Peter and St Paul, where she died. Grieving at their daughter's violent death, Frithewald and Wilburga had her body placed in a lead coffin and carried with great ceremony and public mourning to Aylesbury where it was intended to remain. Strange things happened while the body lay there, including Osyth's ghostly demand that she be returned to her beloved village of Chiche. This was done with all the pomp that this small kingdom could muster, the Bishop of London supervising the placing of her body in a precious casket.

From now on there were tales of miracles, of the sick being cured, the blind given their sight; all who came in supplication to the tomb of Osyth were given what they most desired. As the news was spread abroad, streams of pilgrims came to the quiet village and everywhere it was proclaimed that Osyth was a saint.

The story of the virgin nun is given less credence in these hard-headed days than formerly but it has been recorded that in the 12th century, people going to bed would 'rake up the fire, make a cross in the ashes and pray to God and St Osyth'.

# Coxswain Bloggs
# Hero of Cromer

The resort of Cromer is almost as far north as anyone can go in Norfolk without getting wet feet. Like its sister town Sheringham, a little further west along this bracing coast, it is the chosen destination in summer time of discerning holidaymakers from far and wide. They accept that the town is charming and that the sea in August is properly modest and well-behaved. They forget, perhaps, that the dragon is only asleep and that those who remain in the town in winter months will have to face it when it wakes. Waken it will and when it does another aspect of Cromer is revealed. It becomes a more primitive picture of confrontation with wild forces in which the human element is often displayed with a zeal and heroism beyond any expectation. Cromer has often had to fight the sea and it has done so triumphantly through the courage of that unit of high reputation, that almost mystical band of brothers, the lifeboat crew.

For their support, local people born and bred have turned out on nights of the wildest turmoil at sea to send the lifeboat out and haul it in when it returned. Such an occasion came in the early morning of the 13th of December, 1933, when something like a hundred people braved the bitter cold and drenching spray of a sudden storm to witness one of the most astonishing of all the stories of lifeboat heroism.

In the darkness of that early morning, the sea rose in a fury of wind and water that threatened any craft unfortunate enough to be in its way. At four o'clock in the morning the only powered lifeboat set off in the teeth of the gale to reach a wrecked ship. Its absence was soon to cause a critical situation at Cromer for in the half-light at eight o'clock, the barge *Sepoy* from Dover was driven aground nearby. Though in sight of the watchers on shore and obviously in a desperate plight, the *Sepoy* seemed to be doomed to break up without any hope of assistance.

Then, in a desperate bid to do something, however unlikely its success, the reserve crew of lifeboatmen hauled out the old 'pulling and sailing' boat. With the help of many willing hands the boat was manned and launched into the seething cauldron of the sea. As soon as the boat touched water, the crew pulled on their oar with might and main but the effort was useless. The boat was blown back at once on to the beach. In the shrieking gale it was launched a second time, the crew pulling madly at the oars. For a time the effort was enough to keep the craft afloat but not enough to make headway. As the men tired, the boat was tossed like a cork back on to the beach.

By this time, the forlorn situation of the stricken barge was clearly visible through the spray of mountainous seas. With the decks under water and seas constantly sweeping over the vessel, two men had climbed the rigging and were clinging for their lives in the face of the gale that threatened to pluck them at any instant from their perch.

Desperately, the 'pulling and sailing' lifeboat was launched a third time, but was swept past the barge and thrown again on to the shore. There was no hope that any further launch would succeed. Only the powered lifeboat could have reached the wreck and that was somewhere in the maelstrom of the open sea, probably by now making its way as well as possible to the port of Yarmouth. It was now two o'clock.

An urgent message was sent from Cromer to Yarmouth by telephone and at once the Yarmouth and Gorleston lifeboat was put to sea to intercept the Cromer boat. At eight miles out the two craft met, the message was delivered and immediately the Cromer boat turned about and set off on the 20 mile journey back to its home base. At the helm was Henry Bloggs, most famous lifeboatman of all time. He and the crew had now been at sea for six hours and the gale was at its height.

At Cromer, the barge *Sepoy* had shifted to a position about 200 yards from the shore. Crowds of people who had braved the weather could see the two men still clinging desperately to the rigging of the disintegrating craft. It was three o'clock when the returning lifeboat was sighted and as it approached, Bloggs immediately turned to go to the *Sepoy's* aid and tried to get alongside. Again and again the lifeboat was thrown off by the heavy seas and at some risk to the two seamen, and with little chance of success, a grapnel was used to try and hook the boats together. The sea seemed to take a ferocious dislike to this – the lifeboat was thrown heavily against the side of the barge and holed, then a few seconds later the grapnel line broke.

What else could be done to save the two men? They had endured hours of freezing cold and could not possibly hold on to the rigging much longer. Coxswain Bloggs had to acknowledge that rescue by all the known methods was impracticable in this case; something exceptional had to be done and quickly. After standing off from the barge for a few moments to consider, Bloggs made the decision that was to earn him one of the rare medals of the Lifeboat Institution. With the crew fully supporting him in a do-or-die operation, the coxswain pointed the bows of the lifeboat directly at the barge and advanced full speed to ram the craft. In a grinding crash the bulwarks of the *Sepoy* were stove in and the lifeboat held fast in the uneasy embrace just long enough for three of the crew to leap aboard and drag forward one of the men. The rescuers and rescued man were able to jump into the lifeboat just before it broke away again. There was no thought then, despite the fact that the boat was taking in water through the hole and was damaged in the bows, but to do the operation again for the benefit of the remaining man on the barge. Again the lifeboat came in at speed to ram the vessel. Again the impact and the clasp of timbers held the two together for the few seconds needed. Frozen stiff and frightened for his life, the last man was lifted into the lifeboat just before it broke away.

The job was done. The lifeboat limped to the shore to be greeted by cheers and many helping hands. The crew had endured the most ferocious battering that the sea could produce for seven hours, a long enough day surely for the best of them.

When Coxswain Bloggs first joined the team at Cromer he had been only 18 and he was to spend over 40 years in its service. In 1917 he won the first of his two gold and two silver medals of the Institution, a record that no other person has equalled. He was awarded the OBE in 1924 and received it from the hands of the King on behalf of a grateful country.

It has been recorded that one of the silver medals won by Bloggs was for rescuing a dog. What a story that would make!

# The Downfall
# of Freddie Mann

Freddie Mann was one of those whom we can dismiss
without too much thought. After all, there are so many
people in the world that we can only be expected to remember
those who have something exceptional about them. Freddie
had nothing exceptional so far as anyone could tell, except for
his two bizarre encounters with death.

He had been bright at school, people said, in the only
defence of Freddie that they could think of. You could not help
liking a young boy who was always first to answer questions
and eager to help with the classroom chores. Giving out
pencils and filling up the inkwells was done with a smartness
and dedication that was sadly lacking in his adult life. Of
course, it was only a village school but the teachers were
convinced that Freddie was bound to make something of
himself in the world outside.

What was wrong with Freddie – or with the world – that
they did not seem to get on well together from the moment
that he left school? It was soon apparent that the character
that had flourished in the giving out of pencils in the classroom was unlikely to receive much acclaim in the work
market and his shining morning face was no great recommen-
dation to prospective employers.

For his part, Freddie had resolved to avoid the usual fate of
boys in his situation of labouring on a farm. In the end, from a
vague and romantic idea of wishing to do something con-
nected with the sea, he found a job at Lowestoft helping the
porters and labelling crates of fish. Here, he was only moderately bored and managed to retain a proportion of his shining

aspect to meet and court the pert and pretty girl, Rosie May.

The subsequent marriage was an unhappy one. In the spirit in which he had set out in life to serve rather than to impose, he chose a bride who would make decisions for him and, since she was of a shrewish nature, enforce a petticoat tyranny of ever increasing dominance. There were no children and the couple lived in a slough of discord and misunderstanding, with Freddie seeking sympathy in the bottom of a glass. Inevitably, he teamed up with some of the heavier drinkers at the port and his friendship with the well-known topers, Jimmy Newsome and Ollie Marsh, led to one of the oddest incidents of Freddie's life.

It was a summer evening and the three had walked out of the town to a favourite pub that stood beside a spacious common. It was a particularly jolly evening where memories and resentments were steadily drowned in conviviality. At turning-out time Ollie Marsh found the door first and went ahead to cross the common on unsteady feet, followed by the other two who were giving each other some necessary assistance in the difficult task of keeping the ground steady under their feet. Finding the night air balmy and warm and the grass soft, Ollie decided to lie down and rest. It seemed such a good idea to Jimmy and Freddie that they lay down beside him.

The next morning, Freddie roused up first, stiff and cold and with difficulty awoke one of his companions. The other would make no response at all. It was Ollie, who had lain down first the previous night. The other two deliberated in a hazy fashion and finally decided that Ollie was dead. It was an opinion more expertly confirmed when the constable arrived and officially took control of the situation. Freddie sat down in the grass as he waited and could not help shivering as he realised that he had spent the night next to a dead body.

It may have been this incident that caused a temporary halt to Freddie's back-sliding for in a little while after, he had set himself up with a pony and cart and was in business hawking fish around the villages. It was a heartening success, at least in the early years, and did much to wipe out the feeling of failure that gnawed at his conscience. He had only to ring his bell in a village street and housewives would come out from their doors and indulge in friendly chat, grateful both for the fresh fish and for the break in their loneliness. Perhaps Freddie achieved something of a return to his original bright self in this occupation, picking the fish up early in the morning at Yarmouth and making lengthy rounds in the countryside. The village pubs, however, still exerted their influence and it was not often that he could face the journey home to his contentious wife without some encouragement.

Yet, when some degree of marital freedom came with the couple separating, Freddie was already too far down the slippery slope to recover himself. Too extensive an acquaintance with local ales proved to be increasingly heavy on his pocket and altogether detrimental to the sale of fresh fish. The time came when Freddie had to sell his pony and cart and make do with an aged donkey whose progress was so slow and erratic that only a very limited round was possible and the whole idea increasingly hopeless. Only Freddie's overriding thirst kept him going for a time after he had sold his last fish by virtually begging from acquaintances and those who had seen him in better days. When no drink was forthcoming, Freddie was reduced to performing his special trick for the entertainment of customers in the bar. It consisted in flicking a coin from his foot in the air to be caught in a mug balanced on his forehead. Generally, it was good enough for a half pint of ale to be pushed into his hand.

But, as if fate had determined to defeat Freddie with a final knockout blow, it arranged for even this pathetic trick to go wrong and bring his career to a fittingly ignominious end. One evening, when performing his trick in the bar of the Duke of Wellington, Freddie's unsteady stance caused the tossed coin to miss the mug, enter his open mouth and lodge in his gullet. Three days later he was dead.

From the first, Freddie was lost, like so many of his generation trying to fit a round peg into a square hole. Shining morning face and all, there was nothing particular about him that the world needed and for his weakness he was beaten down and out.

# Searching For Father

Anyone who knows Woodbridge will recognise the obstinate tendency of the river Deben to be at low tide whenever it is decided to take a walk along the river wall. No doubt it has always been so but to the man they called Old Godsend in long ago days, it was no great matter, low tide or not. He walked the river wall as well as the Market Hill and streets around only to be seen and so assure the people that he, the overseer, was present as a faithful servant of the town.

Despite his perambulations he was a pallid man – pale so they said from being so many years in his stuffy office with his nose into everyone else's business. People called him Old Godsend because of his frequent invocations of the Almighty. His importance derived from the control of the town's finances. In those days it was a difficult and always close-fisted operation, with the provision for public care so meagre that one more beggar or one more child born out of wedlock would be enough to turn a shaky balance into a real debt.

Unfortunately, it often happened that when a new birth was put on the register, the father who should be responsible for its upkeep was missing. Either he had hastily departed from the scene or he had only the vaguest identity in the mother's memory – or very often both of these. Godsend vowed that he would have no more of it. The next time that a woman came weeping with a bastard child for the parish to maintain he would turn the county upside down to discover the father and make sure that he paid his rightful dues.

As it happened, that same day a mother and her baby were admitted to the workhouse and, as required by the regulations, the particulars were taken to the overseer, who at that particular moment was in his stuffy office in consultation with

97

the churchwarden, Mr Warne. Mr Warne often assisted in the conduct of parish affairs and he was rather a solemn character since so many of his duties required him to be so and a certain melancholy rested on his features for good and all.

On encouragement from the overseer, who felt that the dignity of his office prevented him from doing so himself, the churchwarden undertook to interview the mother immediately. In as much haste as was seemly the errand was done and the story told. The errant father was a sailor who had been seen a good deal around Woodbridge lately and there was extra evidence in that the baby was considered to be a 'likeness in miniature' of that same sailor. The mother did not know his name but believed he had gone away to Yarmouth.

Godsend weighed up the situation seated at his littered desk where the problems of the poorer citizens were manifest in the untidy papers that barely shifted from one month to another, so conscientious and slow was the overseer in his pursuit of others' deceit. Now at last, it seemed to him, was the time for action. There was additional cause for haste since the sailor was likely to sign on a ship at Great Yarmouth once he had spent whatever cash he had. Whatever it would cost in valuable time and parish funds, this man must be found and brought back to face his responsibilities as an example to others.

With considerably less enthusiasm than the overseer, the churchwarden agreed to accompany him and in fact soon brought in tow a pair of stalwart citizens, one of whom was deputised as a special constable, to complete the party. They would travel by coach next day and search the Yarmouth taverns and other sailors' haunts and if necessary board any of the ships in the harbour to secure their quarry.

It was a very tedious and miserable journey for the quartet on a cold, winter's day and no more could be done after their arrival late in the day than to try and restore something of their original cheer and determination amid the diverting comforts of a good hostelry.

98

Since he knew the man by sight, the churchwarden led the search next day and perhaps with more luck than they deserved in this benighted expedition, the sailor was spotted in only the fifth tavern and immediately confronted. The authority of the Guardians vested in the overseer and the persuasive size and presence of the constable soon convinced the seaman that he was indeed under arrest. At the first opportunity, to wit, the next day, he would be conducted back to Woodbridge to face his responsibilities.

In the meantime, it was hardly necessary for the four of them to stand guard over the prisoner. Allowing himself a feeling of considerable satisfaction if not outright triumph at the early conclusion to the mission, the overseer decided that the duty of gaoler could appropriately be left in the hands of the constable while the three of them sought well-earned relaxation by attending a local play.

The events of that night were to remain in the memories of the overseer and his cronies for the rest of their lives, although always attended by an uncertainty as to what, in sober terms, really happened. It seems that, after the departure of his companions and no doubt very conscious of his new-found importance, the constable kept a close watch on the seaman, allowing himself no more to drink than was reasonable, considering that he and his charge were lodged in a tavern. However, he found it more and more difficult to keep to the role of abstemious official, he being a naturally cheerful fellow himself, when revelling parties came in and full mugs were the order of the hour. There was one particular group of sailors who sought to show their respect for the law by thrusting on to the constable rather more drink than he would otherwise have taken. In fact, the company was so agreeable and his head so hazy that the officer could think of no good objection to a suggestion that they all went to a dance in the town.

From this point there is no doubt that the constable's ability to make decisions rapidly diminished. A very jolly party of sailors brought him back to the tavern around midnight and were so thoughtful of the officer's welfare that they put him to bed and wished him a good night's peaceful sleep before they departed. There he might have lain until daylight brought him to the inevitable realisation of failure, guilt and shame. Before that could happen, though, in the dark and mysterious depths of the night, he was spirited away. No one knew, so they said next morning, how, when or where he had gone. Such things happened in seafaring towns sometimes, when the press gang was lively and when someone tipped them off about a well-built fellow lying half drunk in a tavern.

It was in the small hours, not so long after the constable's disappearance, that the rest of the parish officers returned. Their mood was hearty and convivial and it was noticeable that the overseer was no longer pallid and the churchwarden no longer grave. The jovial atmosphere that enclosed the three and which they obviously wanted to extend to all their fellow creatures, was so well-fortified with local ale that they were unwilling to see anything but good cheer in the appearance of their host in his nightshirt. For some minutes his efforts to explain in sober terms something of what had happened met only with helpless mirth. Then at last the churchwarden seemed to catch the gist of something and reeled upstairs to the room intended to hold both the officer and his captive.

It was empty. The constable was plainly absent and even more certainly was the former captive. In the cold, early morning light, the three adventurers faced the truth. Their plan had gone awry, their triumph turned to failure and disgrace. They had wasted public money and public time on an exercise in which they had made fools of themselves and had actually lost one of their number who, according to the landlord, was by now without doubt on a cutter bound for one of the ships of HM Navy.

In a misery of self-abasement, the overseer decided that the three must leave the inn immediately and start to walk the long journey back to Woodbridge, the town so far away and, in their eyes, so wronged they wondered if it would ever seem the same place again.

Walk they did for many a mile until offered a lift by the driver of a fish cart just south of Lowestoft. The officials pocketed what pride they had left and after an endless journey of deviations and stops on the way, eventually found themselves in the very town of Woodbridge. It was in merciful darkness that the three made their adieux in the market place and made their separate ways home. Surely no one would ever know!

But they would, of course. Misplacing a special constable needed a good deal of justification and was likely to send his wife into hysterics when she heard of it. There was also the cost of the trip to be accounted for and, worst of all, there were sundry travellers who came to lodge at the same Yarmouth tavern and heard the whole story. It was said later that the overseer was never so pompous again nor the churchwarden so solemn but there is no doubt that their nights for ever after were haunted by the memory of their feckless expedition.

# Sammy Day's Place

It is a long time since I visited that part of the Waveney valley where we used to spend our summer holidays. We would go by train to Beccles station and then walk – for an intolerable distance it seemed – into the enveloping country-side. It would take us past the high, grey menace of the old workhouse that seemed so out of place in this rural scene and must have been a constant shadow in the lives of farm labourers living nearby. Then Ringsfield, Barsham and beyond to discover anew each year the timber bungalow where grandfather lived. Now, like most amateur construc-tions of that time, it exists no more.

Whatever its shortcomings, the bungalow was a delight, with its well in the garden, oil lamps for the evenings and the garden in summer with sandy paths and flower beds edged in pungent box. Behind the house there were bushes that drooped with gooseberries and cascades of red, black and white currants.

Beyond the garden was a meadow, so long established that it was very thin as to grass but fairly productive in buttercups and ragwort. It was just the right sort of uncared-for space that might have been created for boys. Even more attractive at the other side of the meadow was a large pond, almost up to the door of the neighbouring house. All this had once been a smallholding and was still known as 'Sammy Day's Place' though Sammy had been dead for many years. Once, he had scraped a living from these few acres with some pigs and chickens and a bit of carpentry on the side. Now, his house-keeper lived alone in the tottering old house.

Inevitably during our holidays we trespassed regularly across the meadow to the pond but never received a rebuke.

On the contrary, the housekeeper seemed to welcome our visits. When we took our jam jars to dredge frogspawn from the pond, she would appear in the top half of the double door, almost filling that aperture with her bosomy presence. I think no one of us ever saw the lower half of that lady for she seldom went out of doors and seemed to be quite contented with her small domain.

On one memorable evening as we fished about the pond, she beckoned from the door and handed out slices of bread covered thickly with beef dripping and smeared yellow with mustard – the most delicious repast I have ever tasted. Good humouredly, she agreed to the pretence that there could be fish in the pond and it only required the right trick of catching them. She would watch us happily as we dipped our bent pins into the water for the hundredth time, until the dusk made shadows all around and bats swooped over our heads. Lamplight would appear in the top half of the house door and throw a soft light for a few yards along the path.

'Better go hoom, yew boys,' she would call and like as not hand us some hoarded cigarette cards or tattered magazines to take home with us. As we went across the meadow we would throw up our hats to try and catch a bat in them but it was an enterprise as little likely of success as fishing in Sammy Day's pond and one of us was sure to lose his hat in the darkness and have to leave it there until next morning. It would be regarded as a happy evening for all that and as darkness drove us indoors it was satisfaction enough to add the cigarette cards and magazines to the collection that we would take home.

Every year we looked forward to our holiday in the Waveney valley and when we arrived we made straight for Sammy Day's Place. If we tired of it we could walk down the sandy 'loke' to the river, no more than a stream with boards reaching from bank to bank. Lying on our stomachs over the water we would catch minnows or sticklebacks. On other days there would be the early clanking of the self-binder to attract us into the fields where we would try to catch rabbits.

Only time defeats such a contented, rustic existence. It was many years later, when the detritus of childhood had become obsolete in the course of our growing up and of changing times, that we disposed of cigarette cards and long-kept copies of the *Magnet*. Among the junk was a school exercise book, no doubt handed to us among magazines by Sammy's house-keeper long before and which had lain unnoticed through the years. There was a scattering of entries in the little book, mostly calculations to do with Sammy's small holding but occasionally changing into prose as if Sammy had half a mind to keep a diary. The most cogent, carefully-written essay among the entries was a description of an extraordinary encounter with primitive superstition in a village nearby. It is best told in Sam's own words:

'About twenty years ago I was returning from a day's shooting by way of a quiet drove known as Bloody Will's Lane, so called in memory of a desperate ruffian that once lived thereabouts – when I was surprised to see a hatless man of past middle age running towards me with an expression of terror on his face I have never seen equalled.

"What's the matter?" said I. Pant, pant. "Oh Lord," was all I got out of him as he sped on his way.

In another second I perceived an ancient female with her grey hair streaming behind her coming in hot pursuit of the man. She had a broomstick in her hand and the way she skimmed over the ground was nothing short of supernatural for her years. My dog, a young pointer, seemed infected with the man's terror and howled dismally.

When I got to the main road I saw a knot of people standing around something that was smoking.

"What's all this about?" I cried.

"It's like this, sir," said an old female party. "That man you saw running – that's my neighbour Bob White. His pigs was ill and he knew they was bewitched by that old Nan Shelton. Well, there was only one way he could cure the pigs as I knew full well. He must get a handful of thatch from the roof of Nan Shelton's house and burn it in front of her door. That would have done the trick, no doubt, but just as he was setting light to the thatch out she comes in a rush from her door. He sets off in a hurry and she after. They came past here like lost souls from hell. Lawks-a-mussy if she do catch up with him there'll be murder done." '

This was the entry in the diary. For all the slapstick spectacle, which Sammy seems to have enjoyed, there is an authentic atmosphere to the tale. The astonishing thing is that such a thing could be told as close to modern times as 1880, when the incident must have taken place.

# The Irresolutes

There was one particular summer's evening at about the time of the Battle of Trafalgar when press gangs were engaged extensively all the way along the coast from the Thames to the Wash. It was a 'hot press' in the popular description. The Navy needed men in numbers and the none-too-gentle persuaders wasted no time in cajoling or trapping single wayfarers, At Yarmouth, for example, where the whole district was scoured for well-set-up young men, the human trawl could sometimes be reckoned in hundreds. In such large operations the method seemed to have been to take all without discrimination, carry them aboard ship or to a well-protected rendezvous on land and wait. In a few hours there would be an outcry in which citizens of varying importance would turn out of their beds to rescue friends, relatives or others.

So it was that the Mayor of Yarmouth was frequently roused in the small hours of the next morning to intercede on behalf of prominent citizens or the Mayor's personal friends. He would be joined in the negotiations by Adjutant Aldred of the Volunteers and by Lieutenant Brown of the Rifle Corps, both of them anxious to retrieve seized men who were already committed to service in the Army. After a lengthy harangue with the navy officers concerned, a fair number of men would be released. For the rest, having little influence anywhere and not among the Mayor's list of friends, they would soon be removed from their familiar hearth and home.

Unfortunately, where the Navy left off, the Army was quick to fill its place. No sooner was the required manpower supplied for Nelson's battles than a massive recruitment began for the military might of the Peninsular War. For this, the Militia provided for the raising of about 75,000 men by ballot.

The ballot was an unhappy compromise for such determined cravens as Steve Bowyer, the Lowestoft grave digger. He had spent much energy and ingenuity in eluding the press gangs and it would be a poor return if he was to be brought into line simply by chance. Bowyer could see that his comfortable grave digging would be uncertain until the choice of men was made. Of course, there was one final let-off, as he knew. If he could persuade a substitute to take his place and provide a sum of £20 or £30 he would still be able to squirm out of military service. Unfortunately, such an amount did not feature in his personal finances or if it did, would have to be wrested from his clutches no doubt with considerable pain.

How many graves Bowyer was destined to dig he could not say but he was on tenterhooks and could not eat or sleep until the day when he was informed that he would not be required for service. He was jubilant. He would be spared the tribulations of the Peninsular War. Then suddenly, in the midst of the self-congratulation, Bowyer was arrested and taken to Ipswich to appear at the General Sessions. Somehow, in circumstances which would reveal a murky commerce in individuals living or dead, he had appropriated a half-a-crown for his own use.

At the Sessions, Bowyer had time to reflect on the fate that brought all his hopes to nought, for he was immediately discharged on condition that he joined the Militia. While he waited for an officer to take him away, he observed another man in the dock, an irascible character named Robert Fields who was charged with failing to keep the peace with his neighbours. It was decided that Fields would be detained until he could provide the necessary sureties as to his future conduct. There was also, it was pointed out, another solution. He was asked: 'How would you like to serve in a man-of-war?'

'How would you?' the man retorted. 'I pay people to do the fighting for me. I don't chose to go.'

At this outrageous attitude the court placed Fields under detention and with ruffled dignity decided that such a man should be dispatched to the Militia.

At one time a quota system was devised by which, foul means or fair, each town and district had to produce a given number of men for the forces. In a certain year Ipswich was expected to deliver 58 men, apparently from the whole area, for each parish and village had to make its contribution. It was by no means an easy task and as the time neared for the completion of the quota there would be urgent advertisements offering substantial financial inducements for substitutes.

In the parish of St Mary-at-the-Key, Ipswich, it was published that a bounty of 20 guineas would be offered to each of 'three spirited young men who will voluntarily step forward to serve King and Country in HM Navy.' Furthermore any one who could produce such a recruit by one means or another would receive two guineas for their trouble.

Serving King and Country was by no means always the first priority of such foot-dragging individuals as Bowyer and Fields, although they were subsequently caught in the recruitment net. Another young man tried a different tack, while just as dedicated to the idea of dodging his responsibilities. He found that his name had been drawn to join the Militia, but because of the system of substitution was able to call on an old friend at Bury St Edmunds to help. The friend was a young married man somewhat overwhelmed with domestic troubles and it took very little persuasion to get him to make the substitution.

As he was a likely young man and physically sound, the authorities had no objection to the change and he was brought before a magistrate to be sworn in. Fear of having too many dependants on the 'strength' had led to the important regulation that a substitute should have no more than one child. When the question was put to him, the substitute replied: 'I have a wife and one child and three in the churchyard.' Perhaps with a suitable expression of sympathy the magistrate thereupon accepted the man as being in all respects a fit subject for the military and so put him on the strength.

Later, when the local Guardians found that they had extra children on the poor rate, the matter eventually filtered through to the army authorities and an investigation showed that the substitute had told the bare but misleading truth. At the time of the oath-taking he had sent three of his very real and lively children into the churchyard to play so that he could satisfy the authorities and salve his own conscience.

# Horse Trading

It was not an isolated advertisement by any means. There were two others on the same page of the local newspaper in similar vein. But it stood out by the detailed description that it carried. It read:

'Thomas Adams, servant to Robert Harper, did on April 28 take his master's Gelding in order to go to North Walsham on his master's business but neither horse nor servant have returned. The information as to the return of either horse or servant to Mr. Harper will receive half a guinea reward. N.B. Thomas Adams was brought up in the Debenham area but knows North Walsham through earlier errands and he is well known for frequenting fairs, being a singer and a player on the fiddle, aged 13 or 14 years. Has his own dark brown hair tied with black ribbon.'

Those people who read the notice in May 1804, probably found no reason to connect it with another terse message relating to a missing girl:

'Mary King went away from the service of Robert Smith of Eyke. She is about 14 years of age, very dark complexion. When found, she is invited to return to her mother who has purchased the remaining term of her service to the above employer.'

In fact, the couple, little more than children, had met at a barn dance at Debenham when Thomas was busily scraping his fiddle to lead the dancers. They found that they shared the same loathing of being bound to long term engagements with none-too-civilised employers and they soon began to talk about the chances of leaving service for a more rewarding kind of life elsewhere. Thomas especially was of an impatient and adventurous nature and felt sure that if he could become released from his indentures he would be able to support himself by his ability to entertain wherever there was a crowd of people.

Perhaps nothing would have come of their ambitions but for Mr Harper's decision to send Thomas to North Walsham to collect some documents regarding the estate of a dead relative. As it happened, both Thomas and Mary hailed from Norfolk, though indentured in Suffolk, and the opportunity to return to their home pastures seemed too good to be missed.

Alternately riding and walking, the couple made slow progress on their journey and were absent for some days before they were missed and the notices posted. They were unaware that Mary's mother had bought her freedom in order to save any further trouble with her employers. It was Mary who later told the story of their misadventures on the way to North Walsham. Apparently the weather was kind as was also the populace in such places as Long Stratton where contributions in appreciation of Thomas's fiddle playing sent them on in good spirits. When they reached North Walsham the fair was in full swing and Thomas was happy to go no further. This was familiar territory and he was confident that he could support himself and follow a more exciting style of life on his own account.

Mary at once went to her home nearby, was received with more sympathy than she had expected and learned that she was now free of domestic bondage to Robert Smith in Suffolk. At the same time she was acquainted with the menacing notice about Thomas's absence and the significance of the reward for his return. For the first time she realised the seriousness of their offence and the danger of Thomas's situation, escaping from his master and with a stolen horse. So far as she was concerned, her relationship with Thomas had ended when she reached her home and she had tired of his volatile moods long before but now with danger approaching for him she felt that she must tell him of the notice and its implications.

Next day she found Thomas at the fair as she expected and tried to persuade him that his bid for freedom could not succeed. He should return immediately to his master and throw himself on his mercy before he was captured or arrested by more violent elements. Thomas saw the danger that he was in but could not bring himself to agree to go back. He had stabled the horse at a back-street hostelry and his decision was now to sell the horse and emigrate, using the money from the sale.

Mary returned to her home aware that she could do no more and soon obtained employment nearby. She never saw Thomas again though she was able to piece together from scraps of letters that came to her in later years, the story of the events that followed.

It was necessary to sell the horse, Thomas decided, as quickly as possible and remove himself to some faraway place where he could start afresh. By now he was acutely aware that his capture could take place at any moment, open to constant surveillance as he was by countless pairs of eyes as he played the fiddle, claiming attention to himself when it was the last thing he wanted. At the very next livestock market in the town Thomas brought his horse to be sold. It was one of many. They were held by their owners or by hired boys, tied to railings or walked up and down as prospective buyers showed interest. Some of the animals were bought and led away but Thomas stood at his horse's head for hour after hour as farmers came up and examined and prodded and passed on. It seemed that the day would end without the horse being sold. At last a man leading another horse stopped and asked the price.

'Thirty pounds,' said Thomas, knowing that his master had once put that price on the horse.

'Well,' said the man, 'my horse is valued at 29 pound. I'll give you my horse and a pound in exchange for yours.'

Desperate though Thomas was to sell his horse, the bargain had no advantage and he refused to be taken in by such a

112

doubtful deal. At that moment there was a touch on Thomas's elbow and a prosperous looking gentleman was standing there.

'Excuse me,' he said, 'but I heard you say that you wouldn't bargain for that horse. Well, I don't blame you. You haven't spent a lifetime with horses as I have. As it happens, that horse is the very one I've been looking for to complete the three that I'm buying today. It's something special, I can tell you. Unfortunately if I approached that man with an offer to buy, since he knows me as a fairly wealthy buyer, the price would double in an instant. Look, I have plenty of money,' and he displayed and opened a leather purse that contained at least 100 sovereigns, 'but I always object to throwing it away. What I want you to do is recall that man and accept the offer, exchange the animals for the one pound profit and the moment it is yours I will buy it from you at a fair advantage to us both.'

Thomas beckoned to the man with the horse, still standing by. In a few minutes the bargain was struck and Thomas waited for the prosperous man to step forward. When he did not do so Thomas searched with dwindling confidence among the thinning crowd. In the end, with one pound and a spavined horse to his credit he was forced to consider the necessity of surrendering himself to his master and praying for his indulgence for all the wrongs he had committed, as a lesser evil than being taken and charged with horse-stealing. The very next day he set out for Suffolk for his master's home.

At this point, with more luck than he deserved, Thomas was dealt a back-hand swipe from whatever fate it is that deals with wayward youngsters and offered a complete, though very painful recipe for survival. He had been scarcely two hours on his journey when he was set on by robbers and relieved of his horse, his papers, his fiddle and one pound. The disappointment of the ruffians at such a small cash reward brought expression in the form of a severe beating, so extreme that Thomas remained unconscious for three days and so secured, however uncomfortably, his safety from blame and punishment.

The attack could not have been more opportune for his pursuers were close behind and would have captured him before he could reach his destination. As it was, the situation of the young boy, robbed and beaten, bereft of his beloved fiddle and lacking most of the clothes he needed for decency, provided a touching, if rather blurred, picture of a loyal servant battling for his life and his master's benefit against a cruel world. With not too many questions asked and Thomas, with his poor memory since the beating, unable to answer anyway, he squirmed out of danger and felt suitably rewarded for his cleverness by being presented with a new fiddle.

# Robert Goodman and his 'Dot and Go'

Robert Goodman stood at the door of his malting shed as the clock in the village struck two and considered his situation. Had he been ill-advised to put down the spread of barley for an illicit malting when it was rumoured that there were Excisemen in the neighbourhood? They had been seen no further away than Fakenham by some accounts while others claimed that there was a group of officers quartered at East Dereham and apparently all prepared to scour the villages around. It was worrying news for Robert but there was nothing he could do about it now. The barley had been spread out and dampened and it was beginning to swell and germinate, already giving off the unmistakable rich aroma of the process. He must trust to his usual good fortune in evading the clutches of the law. In all the years that he had carried out the risky, illegal malting, there had been no more than a couple of narrow escapes.

The particular kind of customs evasion that Robert was engaged in had no connection with the earlier, widespread smuggling along the East Anglian coast. Now, in 1830, official attention had turned to the problem of nefarious brewing. This was even more of a cat and mouse operation with illicit malting often going on under the very noses of the officials. Small domestic brewers, of whom there were many in East Anglia, were allowed to process a prescribed quantity of malt and this only in the actual presence of the law. The officer would be satisfied when he saw the proper amount of barley moistened and started off into germination. Once he was out of sight such wayward brewers as Robert Goodman would set

115

down another quantity for malting. The system was referred to locally as 'dot and go' – the dot being the officially recognised malting and the go the quick, covert operation.

On this fine September afternoon, Robert stood and scanned the road and the countryside around. The very remoteness of his farm and maltings was to his advantage – it was a longish haul from Fakenham and a confusing journey for anyone not used to the area, whether on foot or on horseback. Nevertheless, it was always a nerve-racking time during the illicit malting. The risk of discovery always existed and the punishment for the crime extremely severe.

Only a few days before, Robert's neighbour and confidant, Dodger Warne, had come along with a tale of woe. Although not a brewer himself, Dodger had some sympathy for those in the illegal trade and was shocked at what had happened to his friend Bob Coleman, who had been malting outside the law for many years just outside the village of Stanfield. Unfortunately, Dodger now told Robert, the old man was caught red-handed.

'That happened on'y a few days ago. I was doin' some bark peeling down the lane near my house. Jest as I was a-sittin' down under a hedge to git me breakfast there was a string of about a dozen waggons come along and there was Excisemen in the front. There was a chap a-drivin' the hindermost waggon that I knew by sight an' I arsked him what was a-goin' on.

Tha's that dot and go, he say. They copped this bloke makin' malt when he shou'n't ha' done an' they ha' closed him down.

Well, them Excisemen must ha' took everything that poor owd man owned – malt and wheat, peas and barley, everything he'd got in cereals and provender, legal or not. They was all on the way to the police court in Norwich for the stuff to be forfeited, all on account o' that dot and go. That hardly seem wuth takin' all them risks when you land up in somethin' like that. He'll go to prison as sure as I'm a-standin' here.'

116

Robert wondered sometimes if he was not being stupid and foolhardy but was always persuaded to continue as much for the excitement of the danger as for the rich profits. Today, he was far from sanguine. Perhaps he was getting too old, he thought. He was worried that there were still several hours of daylight left and a sudden and unexpected visit by the Excise was something that could never be ruled out.

It was just after four o'clock, as he was leaving the malting floor for his own quarters that he heard quick footsteps outside and it was Dodger again, filling the office of good neighbour and hoarse with breathless bad tidings.

'There's tew on 'em,' he got out before he sank into the chair that Robert put for him. 'They're a-comin' up this way. They must ha' suspicioned something. I reckon they'll be here afore five o'clock.' He set off again as soon as he had recovered his breath although he had no dot and go to feel guilty about but just felt he wanted to be out of the way of any trouble.

Robert was left in a daze. It was worse and more imminent than anything he had dreaded. Somehow the Excise had become suspicious of his activities and intended to catch him in the act by this surprise visit. Within an hour they would be at the door of the malting chamber and there was no way of pretending that the illicit malting was not going on for it would be spread out in front of their eyes. There was no way to escape being caught like a rat in a trap. He recalled Dodger's story of the other unfortunate dot and go maltster and saw himself ruined, with wagon loads of his property being taken away and himself on the way to prison.

Desperate as he had never been before, Robert realised that only something so extreme and bizarre that it would dwarf the incidence of the malting offence, would be necessary to save him from the dire consequences of discovery. It must be immediate and it must be of an astonishing magnitude to cover the actual crime. There was a way, he thought, looking round the malting floor and it was so mad that it might work. In the centre of the floor a stout, upright beam supported the

117

chamber above where tons of barley were legitimately stored ready for malting. In a frenzy of haste, Robert attacked the beam with saw and axe. Above, the mountain of grain threatened to destroy everything below, probably including Robert himself.

When the supporting beam eventually gave way, Robert jumped back just in time to avoid the thunderous crash as the colossal weight of 100 coomb of barley fell on to the malting floor, filling it several feet thick with grain and bringing down with it timber and weighing scales, pulleys and ropes and hessian sacks in an awesome chaos of destruction. White and shaken but somehow triumphant, Robert leaned weakly against the door and waited.

It was an accident. The Excisemen viewed the vast catastrophe and Robert's visible state of shock and could not believe that so immense a misfortune could be anything but an accident. No one in their right mind would do such a thing deliberately. It was very bad luck. The beam was rotten, Robert told them, he had feared something like this might happen for months past. The Excisemen departed, shaking their heads over the way that fate took a hand in human affairs. It would take a pretty penny to put that lot right again and a pretty long time. There would be no point in coming back until far into the future.

Robert, recovering fairly quickly after the officers had gone, accepted offers of help from many of his neighbours and did not object when a fund was opened for his benefit. In a few months the building was repaired, most of the barley saved and Robert, inveterate gambler as he was, was back in the old business of dot and go.

# New Gaol
# Old Punishments

It was not much of a crime when you came to think about it. Charles Wells had stolen a scythe – at least he was charged with that offence. Charlie denied it with vigour, to the extent of offering to fight anyone that cast aspersions on his character. Somehow, it seemed, he had picked up a scythe belonging to John Syrett, another farm worker. John Syrett had made the most of the mistake, claiming that the scythe was stolen and that he had suffered the loss during the busy harvest. What could have been a simple matter between two farm workers suddenly became an ugly threat.

It seemed to Charlie that the charge was stupid and vindictive. For one thing, one scythe looked very much like any other scythe – it wouldn't be the first time a mistake was made. Anyway he already had one scythe and he had no ambition to keep another. Common sense, he felt, would surely prevail and show how silly the whole thing was.

In the month of September 1791, Charlie presented himself to the magistrates for their judgment. The *Ipswich Journal* described the case in a short paragraph:

'For stealing a scythe, the property of John Syrett of Stowupland, Charles Wells was sentenced to be publicly whipped at the Market Cross between 12 noon and 1 pm on market day and to be imprisoned for 14 days at a House of Correction.'

The severe punishment was a shock to Charlie who had spent nearly the whole of his 30 years oblivious to any existence outside his life on the farm. Suddenly he had been dropped very heavily and he knew that nothing would be the same again. He saw that he would never again be on a

119

comfortable footing with his family, that the village would ostracise him and that the transgression so slight in the beginning would widen little by little as he became a vagrant, forced to beg.

In his fortnight in the cells in Ipswich's New Gaol, Charlie was thrown into frequent contact with another short term prisoner named Noah Barnard. Noah was a character quite different from any of the bucolic acquaintances that Charlie had known. He was a cynical type, a worldly wit who accepted it as natural that he should be a leader. Noah was able to lift Charlie's spirits in his early days of incarceration with a kind of carping good humour.

As it happened, there was a good deal to be humorous about at that particular time. The prison committee had decided to make the New Gaol a proud institution for the county and among the innovations were the gratings, installed in place of windows, that overlooked the street. Probably it was Noah who first saw the possibility of the gratings – in no time prisoners were sitting at the gratings, their legs and arms dangling over the street. Worse still, they occupied their time at their perches in the singing of ribald songs. There was 'considerable annoyance and disgust on the part of respectable citizens' and the practice was quickly stopped.

Released from prison on the same day, Charles and Noah set off together on a tour of Suffolk and Norfolk, begging at farmhouses and stealing only when their stomachs demanded it. From time to time the couple would be rounded up as vagrants and taken back to the familiar confines of the New Gaol.

It was on one of these visits that Charlie and Noah encountered the tread mill. Apparently the consciences of the authorities were aroused when it was discovered how little exercise the prisoners were getting. Mr M Cubitt, Civil Engineer of Ipswich, produced the tread mill, believed to solve the problems of boredom and slothfulness. Certainly a measure of interest was shown by those incarcerated as the tread mill was set up.

On the first day of the experiment, all prisoners, male and female, were told that they would be responsible for working the mill and would be called in shifts to do the exercise. For a short time there was amusement and even enthusiasm for the novelty but as the pointless occupation dragged on, the prisoners protested and ultimately refused to work. All the men present, about 40 in all and many in for serious crimes, swore that they would do the senseless activity no longer, despite being ordered to do so by the guards. Charlie and Noah, hauled in together again for stealing a chicken, watched the pantomime as it proceeded.

First the governor was sent for and he began by cajoling the men and then remonstrating with them. A hard core of prisoners refused to move. The governor then forsook the attitude of sweet reasonableness, picked out 16 ring-leaders and prescribed punishment. They were to be double-ironed, locked in cells on a diet of bread and water and held there until they were properly contrite.

The remainder continued to work the tread mill and of the protesting 16, eleven begged to return to it before the end of the day. Next morning the remaining hard core returned and all prisoners kept the wheel turning without any further objection. If anyone thought of it as useless, since it was not adapted to mill anything, there were no further complaints. The authorities hoped that it would be used to mill flour at some future date.

Charlie and Noah survived the tread mill by the simple philosophy of keeping out of trouble. For a time after that interlude they roamed the countryside together until, without explanation, they drifted apart. Charlie had always been aware that his roots were sunk immovably in the earth and he had precious little satisfaction in the shiftless wandering that their vagrant way of life dictated. When Noah left, Charlie was content to offer his services to a farmer in Norfolk and did not think that he would see his friend again. By coincidence he did so, two years later. He had gone to the market at Kings Lynn on the instructions of his master and while there stayed to watch a line of convicts passing down the street. There were only seven men and heavily shackled.

There was no doubt who was at the head of the seven men. As they rested in their irons against the dock rail, Charlie hailed Noah and heard that the detail was bound for a fishing vessel to sail to the transport ship at Portsmouth and then forward to Botany Bay across the fearful waste of the seas. Noah obviously enjoyed a special reputation among the convicts and even among the guards since he had actually requested to go to Australia. He was hopeful of a new life out there, he said, but his companions were a sorry lot and he did not think they would live through the sea voyage. He wished that Charlie had come with him but said that he would write to him one day if all was well.

Most of the convicts were guilty of larceny and sentenced to 7 years. Daniel Chapman was to be transported for life for burglary and James Horrex for 14 years for stealing a sheep. Charlie watched as the men left the jetty for the open seas and felt a pang that he was not taking this last journey with Noah. In the months that followed he wondered sometimes as he worked on the farm how that rotten ship had fared and whether Noah had survived to reach that distant shore. Two years later he received a letter, directed at first to the village clergyman and then read to him by the clergyman's wife. The letter had been written for Noah before he had died six months before by a woman convict, Susannah Hunt.

Susannah had been transported for robbing the shop of Mr William Notcutt. She had been put on board one of the prison hulks with hundreds of other prisoners in conditions beyond imagining. In her letter she spoke of the excessive cruelty of the captain and although she did not describe particular incidents she let the bare facts of the brutal effects on the prisoners speak for themselves.

Of the convicts on Susannah's ship nearly 400 died on the voyage. Those who survived were generally ill and weak and when they landed they 'died like rotten sheep'. How Susannah survived was something she did not touch on but she gave an account as far as she could of the local people who had gone to Botany Bay with her. John Wiseman, John Lovel, 'Serjeant' Howard were among those who died on the journey. Court-nell, Row and Goodall remained in the hulks. Weavers and Cone were still alive but Cone had been very ill since he arrived. James Riches lived for only a week after arrival. Noah Barnard had struck out for the interior but when he got back to the settlement he was beyond human aid.

# Harry's Wedding

Harry Fulger's life was crowded with excitement. Before he moved from Stowmarket he was ploughing one day in a field nearby when a stranger came cycling by in the lane. When he was opposite Harry, he got off his bike, came to the hedge and shouted 'Stommerget'. Thinking the man said 'stomach ache', Harry pulled up his horses and said he was sorry but there was nothing he could do about it. He was going to add sympathetically that he often had the same trouble himself but the man was waving a piece of paper over the hedge and when Harry went to look he found the name 'Stowmarket'. It turned out that the cyclist was Polish; he had settled in Suffolk after the war but still had difficulty with English pronunciation. Harry obligingly pointed the way. Having directed another stranger only three months before, he felt that he was becoming something of an expert in local geography and often halted his horses when anyone passed in the lane in case they required the benefit of his knowledge.

When other interests entered his life, however, Harry had to consider leaving his job of head horseman at Stowmarket and moving to a similar situation just outside Ipswich. The fact was that he had been courting an Ipswich girl for some years and had lately been persuaded that he could no longer delay the wedding that was his fiancee's right to expect. It was a very unsettling time for Harry. Weddings and such-like social occasions had never entered into his considerations before and the proposed ceremony with all its fripperies promised to be a lot of townish nonsense.

It was not a helpful attitude on Harry's part. A little more concern for the traditional ritual of weddings might have saved him and his bride from one of the most embarrassing situations of their lives, particularly painful since it was fully reported in the *Ipswich Journal*.

Apparently the confusion began on the morning of the wedding day. The bride's father, required to give his daughter away, was missing. A search of all the likely places produced the man eventually but he was in no fit state to attend, let alone take part in the ceremony, having indulged himself rather too well in a premature celebration. Other relations who might have filled the office were also discounted for a similar reason. Harry was reduced to asking an elderly neighbour to perform the task.

'What dew I hev ter dew?' the aged one asked.

Harry was at a loss to explain the correct procedures and merely advised the neighbour to be present and to stand near the bride. 'If the parson ask you anything jest say yes sir or no sir. That's all.'

'Right yew are – I c'n dew that 'thout no trouble.'

By the time the service was due to begin a fair number of friends and relations waited in the church and were rather surprised when the three main participants advanced down the aisle together, none of them quite clear as to precedence. A little late and somewhat fussed and hasty because of it, the clergyman proceeded with the service. By the end of it he had effectively married the bride to the elderly neighbour. No one noticed the mistake and the wedding group moved to the vestry. There, whatever farcical situations might have risen in the future over the mix up were prevented by the revelations of the wrong identities when signing the register. As if stunned, the quartet stared at each other, speechless at the enormity of the error.

What should they do? Perhaps at this point, with his wits about him the aged neighbour could have insisted that what was done was done and claimed his rights. As it was, long minutes passed by while they thought about the matter and meanwhile the congregation, guessing that something was wrong, all crowded into the vestry. There was immediate confusion. It began as a hub bub of talk but quickly became an undignified clamour as the situation was understood. Respectable folk who had sat quietly in the church for the ceremony, now became excessively vocal and aggressive, one family against the other and all against the parson and the old man. Getting himself married to a young girl at his time of life even if it was by accident! What right had he to be there anyway? Amid the shrill cries of females who threatened to faint, Harry's uncle Amos who had travelled from Bury St Edmunds that day especially for the wedding, gave vent to a bellowing laugh. It was immediately extinguished by a swiping blow from a handbag propelled by the bride's mother. Above the cacophony individual voices began to be heard.

'Bishop – the bishop oughter be told.'

'No, nobody can undo a marriage service. That say "he that hath bin joined" '.

'Stand to reason. That can't be changed 'thout some –'

''Thout some sorter allulment –'

'I reckon the bishop should be told –'

'That may well come to divorce in the end –'

The unfortunate clergyman, trying to remember a precedent for such a situation, found himself attacked on all sides almost as bitterly as the reluctant bridegroom who now cringed in a corner. Harry and the bride stood hand in hand in a corner, almost speechless with stupefaction but determined that nothing would separate them, come what may. It was a sight to arouse both pity and courage and the parson needed both to quieten and then address the assembly.

It was a matter of common sense, he told them. A simple mistake had been made and since everyone knew it to be a mistake it could be rectified instantly. The principals had not signed the register and so it was merely logical to have the ceremony performed again immediately, haste being essential to prevent other elements – ahem – from entering into the situation.

As suddenly quiet again as they had been vociferous in the

vestry, the wedding guests filed back into the chancel and, despite the parson's hands raised in protest, actually clapped at the end of the service. Relief returned to worried consciences, the couple kissed as a sign of their unassailable union and the bride's mother walked out of the church with Harry's uncle Amos to show that she had not really meant to hurt him with her handbag. As for the aged neighbour caught up in someone else's romance, he found himself restored to a respectable status by local opinion and went to his home reflecting no doubt on the ephemeral nature of certain married lives.